DERRY
A CITY INVINCIBLE

I dream'd in a dream I saw a city invincible to the
attacks of the whole of the rest of the earth,
I dream'd that was the new city of Friends.

I Dream'd in a Dream

WALT WHITMAN
1819 - 1892

To Melody, Laura and Jane

First Published in 1990
Second Edition 1999
Third Edition 2008
This Edition 2018

(c) Brian Mitchell
(c) Illustrations, Bridget Murray

ISBN 978-0-9515977-0-5

Cover design and illustrations by Bridget Murray.
Typing by Celine Byrne.
Typesetting and design by Simone Horner of
Community Desk Top Publishing Group.
Printed by Coleraine Printing Company.

DERRY
A CITY INVINCIBLE

FOURTH EDITION

Brian Mitchell

Acknowledgements

I wish to express my gratitude to all those authors who have researched and published material on all aspects of Derry's history over the years.

The Local History Section of the Central Library provided a wealth of detail. Thanks to its staff and to Carmel O'Doherty, in particular, for their courteous, efficient help.

The local newspapers proved an invaluable source. The chapters on the '98 Rebellion, Georgian Elegance, A Busy Port and The Troubles were largely put together from reports in either the Derry Journal or the Londonderry Sentinel.

My most sincere thanks to my father for proof-reading the manuscript, to my brother, Peter, for his backing of the project and to Paul Hippsley of Guildhall Press for his guidance through the minefield of publishing.

Contents

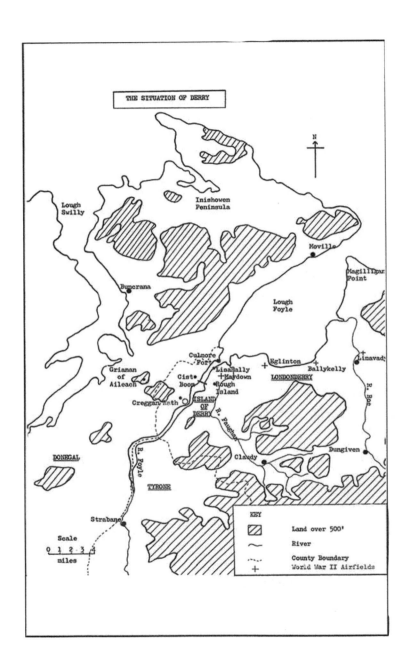

THE SITUATION OF DERRY

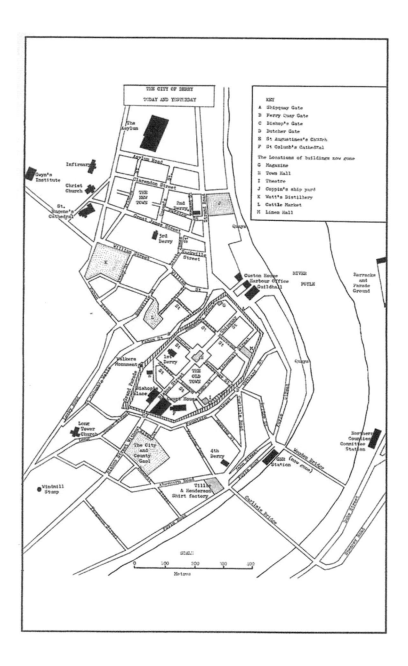

THE CITY OF DERRY
TODAY AND YESTERDAY

KEY

A Shipquay Gate
B Ferry Quay Gate
C Bishop's Gate
D Butcher Gate
E St Augustine's Church
F St Columb's Cathedral

The locations of buildings now gone

G Magazine
H Town Hall
I Theatre
J Coppin's ship yard
K Watt's Distillery
L Cattle Market
M Linen Hall

The Asylum

Infirmary

Gwyn's Institute

Christ Church

St. Eugene's Cathedral

Asylum Road

Clarendon Street

THE NEW TOWN

2nd Derry

3rd Derry

Sackville Street

Great James Street

Custom House
Harbour Office
Guildhall

RIVER FOYLE

Barracks and Parade Ground

Quays

Quays

Walkers Monument

1st Derry

THE OLD TOWN

Bishop's Palace

Court House

Long Tower Church

The City and County Gaol

4th Derry

Northern Counties Committee Station

GNR Station (now gone)

Wooden Bridge

Windmill Stump

Tillie & Henderson Shirt factory

Carlisle Bridge

SCALE

0   100   200   300   400

Metres

Introduction

The story of Derry is one of the most fascinating of any area in Ireland. Her recorded history starts in 545 AD, but there was settlement in the Derry area for thousands of years before that.

As well as having a highly interesting local history Derry, at various periods, played her part in national and international events. In addition to being affected by the events of her time, she made a significant contribution to them. Derry people are proud of their city.

Derry's setting is unequalled: an island of houses climbing a hillside, surmounted by the spires of two cathedrals and brushed by the broad sweep of the River Foyle. Her real strength, however, lies in her sense of community. A very visible expression of this is the phenomenal level of support for her football club, Derry City.

Derry has frequently been described as an overgrown village. This strength of character and community feeling stems, in part, from her history and the knowledge that she is a long-established city. Ask a Derry man about its historical importance and he'll come out with something about St. Columba and a siege. He just knows Derry played her part in shaping history and that he wouldn't want to live anywhere else.

In this book I have attempted to give the broad sweep of Derry's history over the past 4,000 years by tying her story to a framework of sixteen incidents or scenes. Indeed, in the story of Derry we have, in effect, the story of Ireland. Both Gael and Planter made their contributions to the city's development.

Derry has seen turbulent times, experienced prosperous periods when she was a magnet to opportunity seekers, and assumed an importance in Irish affairs far beyond her physical size would suggest possible. Hopefully, the text will give a feel of what it was like to live through these times. The reader can, for example, step into the "civil war" in the city in June 1920; witness captured French soldiers being marched to

Derry jail in November 1798; or stand with fellow mourners at the graveside as Muireartach McLoughlin, High King of Ireland, was buried in 1166 beside the recently constructed cathedral in the monastery of Derry.

It is her history that makes Derry what she is today - a city of character whose invigorating and turbulent past has made her a dynamic city. Sit back and enjoy this time-walk through the history of Derry.

1   The Landscape

Lough Foyle and the Foyle Basin reflect hundreds of millions of years of earth movements and moulding. Encompassed within the Antrim Plateau which culminates in the sheer cliffs of Binevenagh in the north; the rounded peat-covered summits and deeply dissected flanks of the Sperrins in the south; and the rugged series of hills and mountain ranges of the Donegal Highlands to the west, the Lough Foyle basin is a geological time scale.

The Donegal Highlands and Sperrin Mountains represent the western end of a thick belt of sedimentary rocks, deposited in a sea trough, which stretched from what is now Ireland to Scandinavia. About 800 million years ago, under the weight of accumulating sediments of sand (sandstone) and black muds (shale), the trough began to subside. Then 500 million years ago this rock sequence, now 15 miles thick, was intensely folded, heated, crystallised and uplifted into rugged mountain ranges aligned north-east to south-west. This period of Caledonian mountain building reflected the collision of moving plates on which the earth's crust is welded. These plates are constantly being regenerated by volcanic activity at mid-ocean ridges, spreading out and finally being consumed at ocean trenches, generating earthquakes and chains of volcanoes in the process.

By the Carboniferous period, 325 to 370 million years ago, the old mountains of the Caledonian period had been worn away to lie beneath the waves. A warm, shallow sea, similar to the Caribbean today covered Ireland which now lay across the equator. In this sea limy muds (limestone), sand and muds were deposited. What is now Lough Foyle represents a downfold or syncline of the ancient Caledonian rocks which became filled with sandstones and shales of Carboniferous age. Lough Foyle today submerges this basin of Carboniferous sandstone.

Throughout this period the Foyle Basin was in the middle of a vast super-continent called Pangaea, destined to fragment into Africa, the Americas, Eurasia, Australia and Antarctica. Its surface changed continuously. At various times the Foyle Basin was intersected by sea-filled troughs, submerged by shallow shifting seas, crossed by mountain ranges and subjected to climatic conditions ranging from desert heat to equatorial rain and arctic cold.

About 150 million years ago Pangaea began to break up and drift apart. Eighty million years ago the North Atlantic ocean began to form, as America and Greenland were pushed apart. By 60 million years ago the Atlantic was beginning to open right next to Ireland, as the British Isles separated from Greenland. This split was heralded with intense volcanic activity, as basalt lavas flooded out to form the Antrim Plateau, whose western limit now overlooks the Roe valley and Magilligan. At the same time, the earth movements which formed the Alps (as Africa collided with Eurasia) caused the downfaulting and sinking of Lough Foyle along existing north-east to south-west structural lines. The River Foyle, in following the axis of this downfold, also flowed in a north-east direction. The Donegal Highlands and Sperrins, long eroded, were uplifted once again.

By 7 million years ago the Foyle Basin, owing to extensive erosion and drainage development, was beginning to look as it does today. If the general structure was now established, it was the quaternary ice advances, commencing about 2 million years ago and ending 12,000 years ago, which sculptured much of the present detail in the landscape. In fact, much of the detail results from the final retreat of the ice.

During the Ice Age the Foyle Basin experienced climatic fluctuations which caused an alternation of glacial periods, during which the Donegal Highlands and Sperrins were submerged by considerable thicknesses of ice sheets, and interglacials during which temperatures were as high or higher than today.

During the last phase of the Ice Age the Irish ice sheet entered the Foyle Basin through the Glenshane Pass and down the Foyle valley, while an ice sheet from Scotland advanced to the mouth of the Foyle. A variety of drift material was deposited, by both the ice sheets and by their meltwaters as the ice sheets decayed, to clothe and soften the landscape.

Towards the close of the Ice Age a large glacier persisted in the Foyle valley after the northern slopes of the Sperrins had become ice-free. The River Faughan, dammed by this glacier, became a massive lake. Likewise the River Roe, in the stretch from Dungiven to Limavady, became a great lake in front of the southern limit of the Scottish ice. In these lakes extensive thicknesses of sand and gravel were deposited. Glacial drainage channels were carved out, acting as overflow channels for the ice-dammed lakes. The River Faughan was forced to turn northwards along the eastern margin of the valley glacier.

As the Foyle glacier downwasted and retreated southwards its meltwaters carried large quantities of sand and gravel, which were deposited as extensive outwash terraces along the shores of Lough Foyle. On the lower reaches of the Faughan, at Ardlough, kettle holes were left behind as masses of ice, buried under the outwash deposits, melted. With the ice gone, this outwash material became a 50 feet terrace along the shore of Lough Foyle, as the land level rose in adjustment to its lighter, ice-free load.

The island of Derry owes its isolation to the Foyle glacier, as meltwaters flowing beneath it carved out the deep channel to the west of the hill.

Culmore Point and Magilligan Point had their origins in post-glacial times. They are both sand spits. The latter is an enormous flat triangle of river-borne alluvium and wind-blown sand.

When man first reached the Foyle Basin, perhaps in about 6,000 BC, this was the landscape which confronted him. Only one piece of detail is missing. He would have found a land forested everywhere. As the climate improved, with the retreat of the ice, forests of willow and birch, followed by hazel, pine, alder, oak, elm and ash replaced the sparse alpine flora.

This is the landscape which man in the Derry area had to deal with. Compared to the geological forces which created the Foyle Basin, man seems rather puny and very inexperienced. Man has been around these parts for 8,000 years which, in geological terms, is just a blink of the eye.

2   The Bronze Age

One Autumn's day in 1987 a local farmer ploughing his hill-top field, overlooking the River Foyle, hooked a large flat stone, of dimensions 5 feet by 4 feet, and brought it to the surface. There it remained while the winter's frosts worked to break up the soil. It was members of Shantallow Local History Society, out searching for flint fragments, the evidence of prehistoric settlement, who on coming across this large flat stone realised it was perhaps the capping stone of a Bronze Age grave. The Archaeological Branch of the Department of the Environment was called in, who, on one very wet March day in 1988, carried out an emergency dig.

What they found convinced them that here in the townland of Shantallow, on the fringe of the present-day city of Derry, in the early years of the second millennium BC, lived a small village community of farmers who had trade connections with the flint-mining areas of County Antrim, and who in a nearby cemetery buried their dead.

The stone which had lain undisturbed for some 4,000 years was, in fact, the capping stone of a cist tomb. Around 2,000 BC a circular pit, 4 to 5 feet deep, had been dug on the brow of a small hill, 250 feet above the River Foyle. In the middle of this pit slabs of stone had been laid on edge to create a stone box, 4 feet long by 2 feet wide. The corpse, with his or her knees folded up to its chest, had been placed in this coffin on its side. Only part of the skull and part of the leg bone remained of this skeleton, as the rest of the body had rotted away through contact with the soil. Behind the neck of the corpse was an earthenware pot in the shape of a bowl and decorated with jagged imprints. This bowl had been made specifically for the burial ceremony. It is clear that these people believed in some form of afterlife, as the bowl would have been filled with food or drink to sustain the body after death in the journey through the underworld.

The cist in which the corpse lay was then roofed with a capstone. In this case, as occurred on other sites, the grave wasn't marked above the ground with a mound of earth. The farmer had inadvertently uncovered on this hill-top site a Bronze Age cemetery.

This distinctive form of burial, in a short cist with an upright bowl-shaped food vessel, is not unique to Ireland. It has been found all over Europe, even as far east as Russia. It represents the spread of the so-called Beaker peoples, named after their pottery, who originated in lands around the mouth of the Rhine, then spread to Northern Britain and from there to Ireland. Around the early years of the second millennium they had reached Shantallow.

These people were settled pastoralists who introduced metal-working into Ireland. Near the cist in Shantallow fragments of flint, which is not a native rock of this area, were found, and the area of their greatest concentration marked the spot where a small community lived. Shantallow clearly supported a Bronze Age village. The flints were fashioned to be used as arrowheads and thumbscrapers. The arrowheads would have been used in hunting while the thumb-shaped flint scrapers would have been used in the preparation of animal skins before they were cured. Clothes would have been made from this leather.

No metal artefacts were found, but in other cist burials hundreds of metal implements have been found. Ireland possessed abundant supplies of copper, and these people exploited in a large way Irish copper and gold, as evidenced by the metal axes, knives and daggers they left behind. Their most outstanding personal ornament was the sheet-gold lanula, a crescent-shaped neck ornament.

The settlers at Shantallow were primarily livestock farmers. With their metal axes they would have begun to clear some of the surrounding forest to expose good pasture land. Here cattle were grazed for their beef. They would also have grown wheat, oats and barley, with the grain being ground on saddle-querns.

Within an earth enclosure, perhaps topped with a palisade of timber stakes, the early inhabitants of Shantallow would have lived in small, single-room, circular wicker huts. Their houses were probably built of posts and wattle rods. Strong posts were driven into the ground, and thin saplings of hazel, elm or ash were woven between them to form the walls. Then the walls were plastered with daub in which mud was mixed with straw. This mixture dried very hard to create a sturdy homestead. The roofs would have been thatched with straw or rushes obtained from marshy ground.

Our early settlers at Shantallow would have only made a small impact on the forests which clothed this area. Only the hill top would have been cleared of wood.

On a clear day, rising above the trees that swept down to the banks of the Foyle on both sides of the river, the early dwellers of Shantallow might have spotted, some two miles to the south-east across the river, smoke curling up from open hearths on Rough Island in Enagh Lough. Finds of late Stone Age and Bronze Age pottery fragments on this island, lying almost in the middle of the lake, roughly circular in shape, with a diameter of 150 feet and now largely overgrown with trees and shrubs, identifies this as a settlement site around the same time as the community of Shantallow were burying one of their members.

This site on Enagh Lough, termed a crannog, was formed by a platform of timber, overlain with a layer of packed stones almost 3 feet deep, being placed, timber by timber and stone by stone, on top of a marshy island created by glacial dumping during the last Ice Age. Bronze spearheads, flint flakes and abraded stones, worn away by man's rubbing or scraping, attest to its settlement in prehistoric times.

Around the edge of the crannog there may have been a defensive palisade of timber stakes with lighter branches of wattle woven in and out through them. The houses inside, built of wicker, wattling and daub, and the lifestyle would have been very similar to those at Shantallow. Barley, wheat and oat impressions found on the pottery fragments are evidence of the cultivation of these crops in fields around the shore of Enagh Lough. In addition to farming their own food, the inhabitants here exploited the fish and fowl associated with a small lake.

No names or even exact dates can be identified against these Bronze Age settlers of the Derry area. But we do know that they did exist, and that they began man's first tentative exploitation and alteration of the local environment.

3   *Colum Cille*

In 545 AD, according to the Annals of Ulster, the church of Doire Calgach, "the oak wood of Calgach", was founded by Colum Cille (Columba). Whether Derry was more than an oak grove before this is a matter of conjecture. In 71 AD Agricola began his northern campaign to extend Roman control into Scotland. He was met by a confederation of Britons, Picts and Irish, led by Galgacus, who in a great battle defeated the Roman army, and thus prevented their penetration into the Scottish Highlands. Could Galgacus be an Irish king whose headquarters were on the island of Derry? There is no doubt that from the 1st century AD a wave of Celts, called Scots, went over from Ireland to Argyll and founded the first Celtic Kingdom of Scotland, Dal Riata. At first Dal Riata was an extension of a northern Irish kingdom of the same name on the north Antrim coast. With Irish kings claiming lordship over this Scottish kingdom it was only natural they would defend it in times of attack.

Christianity had come to Ireland one hundred years before Colum Cille founded his first monastery in Derry. When St. Patrick landed in Ireland to convert her to Christianity in 432 AD it was to the royal fort, in each district, he approached. Having converted the king, the people followed his example. So in 442 AD St. Patrick arrived at the royal palace of Grianan of Aileach, a stone cashel within three concentric earth enclosures, 800 feet above sea level, on a hill commanding entry into and out of Inishowen, County Donegal. Here he converted Eoghan (Owen), son of Niall of the Nine Hostages, who had been High King of Ireland from 378 to 405 AD. By the time of St. Patrick's death in 465 the whole of Ireland was Christian.

The early organisation of the Irish church, introduced by Patrick, was diocesan, and each diocese was under the jurisdiction of a bishop.

However, this system proved incapable of adaptation to Ireland's tribal system. By the 6th century its place was taken by monasteries, each under the control of an abbot, and each acting as the religious centre for the area. Each clan now had its own church and clergy. Land was allotted to the clergy for their support, and the clergy lived together in communities clustered round a church.

Colum Cille was in a favoured position to benefit from this tribal patronage. Born in 521 at Gartan, County Donegal, Colum Cille was of royal descent, his great-grandfather being Conall Gulbhan, son of Niall of the Nine Hostages. As kingship rested within the family group known as the *derbfine* (made up of all those males who had a great-grandfather in common), Colum Cille was entitled to be considered for chieftainship of the Cenell Conall, whose territory covered County Donegal west of Lough Swilly.

Ainmere, King of Ireland at the time, was Colum Cille's cousin, and it was he who gave the island of Derry as a gift to Colum Cille on which to found a church and school. It was an ideal spot for a monastery, secluded yet convenient. Derry was then entirely surrounded by water. The Foyle divided south of the island, the main stream running on the east side, while a small volume flowed in a shallow river on the western side, rejoining the main stream to the north.

A small self-sufficient monastic community was soon established. This first monastery at Derry would have been built within a perimeter earthwork which acted as a symbolic boundary between the monastery and the secular world rather than as a defensive structure. Inside, the principal building was a rectangular wooden church or oratory. The walls were either of wattle and daub, or of sawn oak planks. The roof was high-pitched, and it was either thatched or made of shingles, i.e. slates made of wood. The church would have been small, perhaps no longer than 15 feet internally. Around the church the monks would have lived in small beehive-shaped huts, made of wattle, which were located higgledy-piggledy amongst the oak forest. There would have been a variety of other simple buildings - all made of wood or wattle with thatched roofs. In a scriptorium, or writing hut, Colum Cille and his monks would have made copies of psalters and the Bible. There was a school to prepare boys for the religious life. A library was essential for such a centre of learning in which Latin grammar and classical books would have been kept. The scriptorium, in copying books, preserved early classical and

Christian writings for use in the school and library. The monks and pupils were fed in a common refectory. There would have been a guest house for the pilgrims who visited during major festivals. There would also have been a royal house where the rulers who patronised Colum Cille could stay when they visited. There were timber crosses, probably set in milling stones, which acted as focuses for prayer and meditation. A monastery controlled extensive lands and a large tenantry outside its earth enclosure. At the river shore there would have been a boat-house to facilitate the ferrying of visitors across the Foyle. From their coracles, made of animal skins stretched over wickerwork frames, the monks fished for salmon and trout.

The monks' day was divided into periods of labour and prayer. The fields near the monastery had to be tilled, with oats and barley to be sown and harvested. The herds of cattle which grazed on the open pastureland had to be watched, as did the pigs and sheep left to browse through the oak groves. In the wood, wattle for building purposes had to be gathered. The monks, as they went about their work, could be easily distinguished from the tenantry by their tonsure, in which the front of the head was shaven from ear to ear.

Outside the monastic complex farmers lived in circular raths such as the one at Creggan. These farmsteads were formed by digging a ditch, the earth being thrown up to form a bank which was topped with a wooden palisade. Inside the circular enclosure, usually from 70 to 150 feet across, breached by a causeway which led through a gate, the farmer housed his family and animals. The enclosure had no real military significance, but it offered sufficient protection against small bands of marauders and wolves. In the small, one-room, circular wooden huts with thatched roofs the farmers' families lived, cooked and slept. Beds were simply piles of straw. The common form of dress was a short linen tunic worn underneath a long woollen cloak, fastened by a brooch.

During the day the farmer's cattle and sheep were left to graze on the open pastures, while at night they were safely housed from wild animals and thieves in pens within the rath. Cereals, mainly oats and barley, were grown in small fields, no more than two acres in size, close to the dwelling. The corn was then ground in small rotary querns (an improvement on the earlier saddle querns) within the farmstead. Food was cooked on an open fire, with a spit being used for roasting and a big cauldron, made of sheet metal, for stewing.

Within a short space of time Colum Cille's monastic foundation at Derry had become a centre of considerable wealth, learning and population. The island of Derry now supported a thriving religious and farming community amongst clearings in the oak forest which formerly clothed the whole island.

4 The Vikings Come

"From the 6th to the 10th century, while the peoples of Europe were torn asunder by internal struggles and racial wars, Ireland and Ireland alone of all the nations kept the light of faith and knowledge alight and burning with a brightness which diffused its rays far beyond the shores of Erin."

One of the most striking features of early Irish Christianity was the love of wandering in order to pass ones life in solitude. As a consequence of this quest the Irish became great missionaries. In 563 Colum Cille set sail from Derry to found a new monastery. Conall, 6th King of Dalriada, granted him Iona, a small island off the west coast of Mull. This was to become the mother house of a confederation of Columban monasteries throughout Ireland, Scotland and England.

In the century following Colum Cille's death in 597, new monasteries were founded at Lindisfarne in Northumbria, Rathlin Island, Innisboffin (County Galway) and in the lands of the Picts in Scotland. In addition to Colum Cille's own foundations at Derry and Durrow, these monasteries all looked to Iona as their leader. They adhered to the traditions of the Irish church. These Columban monasteries played a leading role in the expansion of Christianity; they converted the Picts and restored Christianity to Anglo-Saxon Northumbria in the 7th century.

In the second half of the 8th century Iona was at the height of its prestige - the laws of Colum Cille held sway in Ireland, with the abbots of Iona making frequent trips there. This period of Columban expansion resulted in the appearance of two art forms to Irish monasteries; namely, high crosses and illuminated manuscripts.

The fusion of Irish techniques of timber construction and Northumbrian skills in stone carving resulted in the appearance of highly decorated standing crosses in Irish monasteries from the second half of the 8th century. These elaborate high crosses with the wheel head design, in which a circle surrounded the point of intersection, developed from the earlier simple pillar stones of the 6th century on which crosses were incised. In the monastery at Derry there would now have appeared intricate high crosses on which scenes from the Bible were sculptured. The purpose of the crosses varied. Some marked burials, others signified a boundary of some sort, while others acted as focuses of prayer.

Distinctive manuscripts on parchment were now being produced in Columban monasteries. Sometime between 760 and 820 the Book of Kells, a brilliantly illuminated copy of the four gospels with Latin text, known as "the Great Gospel of Columkille", was written. Its precise origin is unknown; not every monastery could produce such highly decorated and, at the same time, legible and correct copies of gospels written in Latin. Undoubtedly it was written in a Columban monastery, as they were famed for their teaching of Latin and the classics and for the skills of their craftsmen and artists. It was unlikely to have been written in Derry, as the team of scribes and artists required to produce such a masterpiece probably only existed at the monastic centre of the Columban confederation, which was Iona to 806 and subsequently Kells in central Ireland.

The contents of the 8th century library and scriptorium at Derry have not survived. Colum Cille, according to the Annals of Clonmacnoise, wrote 300 books, all copies of the New Testaments. Copies were left with each of his churches, which, of course, included Derry.

The earliest surviving decorated Irish manuscript is the Cathach or Battle Book, a copy of the psalms, which according to tradition was written by Colum Cille towards the end of the 6th century. It was handed down in the family of Conall Gulban, i.e. Colum Cille's kin, and it was always carried three times round the army to ensure victory before they went into battle. Illumination in this manuscript was confined to the fine large capital letters at the beginning of each psalm.

With the Book of Durrow, a copy of the four gospels written in the mid-7th century, an Irish style had emerged in which at the beginning of each gospel there was on the left a full ornamented page, brilliantly coloured, with intricate designs of spirals and interlocking animals and plants; while on the right there was an introductory page beginning with a large, beautifully proportioned, capital letter. In addition, portraits or symbols were used to depict each of the four evangelists.

The Book of Kells marked the pinnacle of Irish achievement in manuscript production, with its profusion of illustration, colour and ornamentation, and its repeated use of the same symbols for the four evangelists; a man for Matthew, a lion for Mark, a calf for Luke and an eagle for John. By the end of the 8th century the monastic settlement at Derry would have changed little. The monastic complex would still have been made of timber. The only new physical feature would have been the erection of a few high stone crosses. The scriptorium may have begun to produce some basic illuminated manuscripts, similar to the Cathach. It would, of course, have continued to make straight copies of the psalms and gospels.

In 812 a fleet of ships, the like of which had never been seen before, sailed up Lough Foyle. These ships, built of oak, some over 70 feet long and 20 feet wide, and steered by a rudder paddle, were powered by both oar and sail. From 40 feet pine masts fluttered square sails of double-thickness strips of red and white woven cloth, and, from behind rows of shields slung over the side, men, up to 32 on each boat, pulled on narrow-bladed spruce oars and manoeuvred the boats into the sheltered waters of the River Foyle. They beached their boats, which drew only 3 feet of water, on the shore beneath the monastery. From the boats men rushed up the hill, the leaders wearing protective coats of mail and helmets with a nose piece which projected down over the face; the rest, following close behind, in thick woollen coats which reached half way down their thighs. They all carried a round wooden shield, many of which were painted either yellow or black. The long, broad, two-edged iron sword and the long-handled, broad-edged battle axe were the principal weapons they carried. Some were armed with spears, others with bow and arrows. Most had an iron knife, with a wood or bone handle, tucked in their belts.

The Vikings had located the monastic settlement at Derry, and, as elsewhere in Ireland and Britain, they met no organised resistance. They burnt the abbey and massacred her clergy and students. Not only was the monastery an easy target to attack because of its secluded, yet very accessible, location, it was also a very rewarding one. Derry was a centre of wealth, rich in lands and livestock. The Vikings were interested in food provisions, to sustain further voyages, as well as in the precious metal ornaments associated with a monastery. They were also interested in taking prisoners, especially girls, as they had been trading in human slaves to central Europe for centuries.

The Vikings never attempted to settle in Derry. In 832 they again attacked, but this time they were driven back, with great losses, by Niall Caille, King of Ireland and Murchadh, Prince of Aileach. Derry continued to be attractive to Viking invaders throughout the 10th century. In 983 the shrine of Colum Cille was carried away by the Vikings. In 989 and 997 she was again plundered.

Derry's long-term growth did not suffer because of the Viking raids, if anything it increased. With the Viking raids on Iona in 795, 802 and 806, the monks acquired a site at Kells in central Ireland, and, bearing the relics of Colum Cille, moved there to found a new monastery. There was a steady rise in the status and importance of Derry from 900, as she succeeded Iona and then Kells as the centre of all Columban foundations in Ireland and Scotland. By the end of the 10th century Derry was known as Doire Columcille, as opposed to Doire Calgach.

This Viking period resulted in two new additions to the monastery at Derry: her first stone church and a round tower. Sometime after the first raid in 812, the wooden church, which the Vikings burnt, was replaced with a stone one. It would have been a simple building, similar in shape to its wooden predecessors. This stone single-chamber church, later known as Dubh Regles or Black Abbey church, was perhaps no longer than 20 feet. It probably had one narrow slit for a window, and was roofed with stone to simulate overlapping tiles. Housing for the monks and their tenant farmers was still made of the traditional wood and wattle combination.

Sometime between the end of the 10th century and the beginning of the 12th century, a round tower of stone was built next to the Black Abbey church to serve a variety of purposes, such as a belfry, a watch tower and a place of refuge. Perhaps 100 feet high and 15 feet in diameter, with five floors, each lit by one window except the top which had four, entrance was gained, 10 feet above ground level, by a movable ladder. Inside, each wooden floor was linked by a wooden staircase. If set on fire this tower would have been a death trap, as the up-draught working on ignited wooden floors would have created an inferno.

By the turn of the 12th century Derry was beginning to see a revival in its fortunes as an important monastic town. Apart from the additions of elaborate stone crosses, a small dry-stone church and a round tower, Derry was still very similar to the settlement founded in 545.

5   The High Kings of Ireland as Patrons

It is no coincidence that the resurgence of Derry as a monastic centre coincides with the rise of the MacLoughlins as contenders for the High Kingship of all Ireland. In the 12th century the MacLoughlins were the leaders of the Cenel Eoghan, from their royal palace at Aileach.

A monastery was seen as an integral part of a ruler's prestige, and it was closely identified with him because it was he who endowed it with its landed wealth. It is not surprising, therefore, that monasteries, with their valuables, surplus food and herds of cattle, became targets for attacks during feuds between local rulers.

Derry's fortunes were now attached to those of the MacLoughlins. For some 30 years Domhnall MacLoughlin, King of Aileach, fought with Murchertach O'Brien, King of Munster, for recognition as the High King of Ireland. In 1088 Domhnall invaded Munster, and destroyed the royal palace at Kincora. In 1094 Domhnall was recognised as High King when all the rulers of Ireland came to Aileach to pay tribute. In 1100 Murchertach O'Brien marched north, and destroyed the fort of Aileach. Soon afterwards O'Brien was defeated by the grandson of Lochlainn, Lord of Inishowen.

After 30 years of indecisive struggle Domhnall MacLoughlin retired to the monastery in Derry to spend the last few years of his life in prayer and contemplation. In 1121 Domhnall, described as King of Aileach for 11 years and as High King of all Ireland for 27 years, died aged 73. All the chiefs of Ireland assembled in Derry for his burial in the graveyard by the Black Abbey church.

The local chiefs regarded the monastery of Derry as sacred. The O'Kanes of the Cenel Eoghan had donated land to the monastery, while the O'Dohertys and O'Maldorys of the Cenel Conall had provided gifts

25

of chalices for the religious ceremonies.

In 1148 Muireartach MacLoughlin, son of Domhnall, was recognised by the O'Neills as King of Aileach, and in 1159 by Rory O'Connor, King of Connaught, as undisputed High King of Ireland. Muireartach was slain in battle in 1166.

Meanwhile, in 1158, Flahertagh O'Brolchain was appointed as "successor of Colum Cille", Abbot of all abbeys under the rule of Colum Cille, including Iona. He began preparations for the erection of a new cathedral in Derry worthy of its distinguished founder. A visitation through the lands of the Cenel Eoghan returned with livestock and gold sufficient to fund the work.

In spring 1162 a big clearance scheme was begun under the personal direction of Muireartach MacLoughlin, then High King of Ireland, and the Abbot of Derry, Flahertagh O'Brolchain. Eighty houses adjacent to the Black Abbey church were demolished and their debris cleared away. A circular stone wall was then built around the cleared area. In 1163 a limekiln, measuring 70 feet square, was constructed by the clergy of Derry in 20 days close to the River Foyle, where there was an abundance of sea shells for making lime. All the best craftsmen from Counties Derry, Donegal and Tyrone were summoned to Derry. Trees were cut and brought up to the stone enclosure where lime and stones were already piled. In 1164, in the space of 40 days, Templemore or "the Great Church" was built near the original abbey. As befitted a settlement which had the patronage of Muireartach MacLoughlin, High King of Ireland, and which was head of all Columban monasteries, Derry now had one of the biggest cathedrals in Ireland, measuring 80 feet in length. Compared to Continental cathedrals of the time it was a simple structure, perhaps with a nave linked by an arch to a chancel with a few simple but decorative round-headed windows.

In the mid-12th century there were attempts to revive Iona as a great monastic centre. In 1164 the community of Iona came to Derry to offer the position of Abbot of Iona to Flahertagh O'Brolchain. They were unsuccessful, as the local rulers, patrons of the monastery in Derry, would not permit it. In 1203 a more radical attempt to restore Iona's status saw the erection of a Benedictine monastery. In 1204 the abbots of Derry and Armagh, together with monks from Derry, sailed to Iona and pulled down this monastery. The Abbot of Derry, with authority over all Columban foundations in Ireland and Scotland, could not sanction such a monastery on lands belonging to the Columban community.

In 1175 Flahertagh O'Brolchain died in the Black Abbey church. Derry was now a centre of pilgrimage and a haven for the privileged to retire to in preparation for death. In 1196 Muireartach, son of Muireartach MacLoughlin the High King of Ireland from 1159 to 1166, Lord of Cenel Eoghan and royal heir to all Ireland and "dissolver of the foreigners and upholder of churches", was killed in battle by Donoch O'Cahan and carried to Derry and buried there.

At the dawn of the 13th century Derry was still going its own way, following on the traditions of Colum Cille, despite the fact that the rest of Ireland was conforming to the diocesan organisation and accepting the new religious orders of Continental Europe.

Around 1230, however, the old Columban foundations in Derry were taken over by the Augustinian order. This Augustinian monastery was very wealthy, as they possessed lands in Counties Derry, Donegal and Tyrone. A Cistercian convent of nuns was founded in 1218 on the south side of the island of Derry. They were endowed with gardens and homesteads on the west bank of the Foyle and with woods on the east bank. On the north side of the bog near the island, a Dominican monastery was built in 1274 under the patronage of the O'Donnells, chiefs of Tir Connell. One hundred and fifty friars lived and worshipped here.

In 1281 Donnell Oge O'Donnell, Lord of Donegal, was defeated and killed in battle by the army of Hugh Boy O'Neill, Lord of Tyrone. His body was brought to Derry, and it was buried at the Dominican abbey in "the monastery of the friars".

With the new religious orders came more elaborate churches and monastic complexes. Abbeys were now erected where the entire community lived under a single roof, as opposed to the cluster of cells around the old churches. The Dominican Priory was a castellated building of four storeys high flanked by square towers at each corner. The Cistercian nunnery was probably typical of other small 13th century nunneries. A church with a nave, chancel and choir occupied one end of a square cloister, while stone buildings completed the other three sides. Here the nuns could worship, study, sleep, eat and contemplate without stepping outside the nunnery. A library, refectory and dormitory were all contained within the complex.

The oak grove was still quite extensive on the island, as it was recorded in 1178 that "a violent storm prostrated 120 oaks in Derry Columkille".

The resilience of Derry was striking. The monastery and community were plundered and destroyed countless times in the early 13th century, yet the new religious orders came to Derry. In 1197 MacEtigh from the Keenaght robbed the altar of the great church of Derry, and carried off the four best goblets in Ireland. He broke the goblets and took off their jewels before he was captured and hanged at the Cross of the Executions. In 1203 Derry was burned from the cemetery of St. Martin to the well of St. Adomhnan. In 1204 Diarmait MacLoughlin was killed and his army defeated when they plundered the shrine of Colum Cille. In 1211 the sons of Randal MacDonnell came with a fleet of 76 ships, plundered and destroyed the town, before passing into Inishowen and laying waste the whole peninsula. The town was again plundered by the MacDonnells in 1213, when they carried off the treasures of the cathedral to Coleraine. In 1215 Hugh MacLoughlin carried off the herd of cattle belonging to the monastic community. In 1222 Derry was yet again plundered, this time by Niall O'Nial.

It was evident that the monastic settlement in Derry still relied on the patronage of the local lords. Kings continued to be buried here and the clergy still retained their tribal loyalty, as witnessed by the killings in 1261 of sixteen of the clergy of the Cenel Conall in Derry by Conor O'Neill. In the 12th century the MacLoughlins, Kings of Aileach and contenders for the High Kingship of Ireland, were the main patrons of the monastic community in Derry, while in the 13th century it was the O'Donnells, Lords of Donegal.

By 1300 Derry was a very impressive monastic settlement. Beside the old Columban foundations of the Black Abbey church and the cathedral, now taken over by Augustinian canons, was the royal burial ground marked by recumbent and upright grave slabs. In the new complexes of dwellings and church under one roof the well-ordered lives of the Cistercian nuns and Dominican friars went on. And towering above them all, and seemingly piercing the sky, stood the round tower.

When the English expeditionary force landed at Derry in 1566 they interrupted the pattern of life of the three religious foundations - Augustinian, Cistercian and Dominican - established over three centuries. By 1567 their buildings lay empty and in ruins. Today there are no physical remains of Derry's one thousand year history as a monastic settlement. The link with the monastic period is only retained in the name Long Tower, which refers to the round tower of the monastery which formerly stood here.

6   *Strategic Outpost*

Owing to Derry's central position between the two most powerful
kingdoms of the O'Neills of Tyrone and the O'Donnells of Donegal, it
was only a matter of time before the Tudor rulers, who since 1534 had
been attempting to bring Ireland under English law and rule, would
attempt to fortify Derry. For a while in the early 14th century it looked
as if the Normans might gain a foothold. In 1305 Richard de Burgo built
a castle at Greencastle to protect the approaches to Lough Foyle, while
in 1311 he was granted Derry. By 1333, however, there was no Norman
presence west of the River Bann.

The clans of the Derry area were well established in their respective
territories when the English armies began to encroach in the 16th
century. The O'Neills were the chief family of the Cenel Eoghan, their
territory comprising Tir Eoghan (Tyrone), and they were overlords of the
province of Ulster. The O'Hagans, from their seat at Tullahogue,
exercised the hereditary right of inaugurating the O'Neill chiefs. The
O'Hegartys, from their base in Loughinsholin barony, were sub-lords to
the O'Neills.

The O'Donnells, the rulers of Tir Conaill (Donegal), had risen in
predominance in the 13th century at the expense of the McLoughlins,
who had been the most powerful sept in Donegal and, indeed, in all of
Ireland in the 12th century. The O'Gallaghers, from their territory in the
baronies of Raphoe and Tirhugh, acted as marshals in O'Donnell's armies
from the 14th century. The O'Dohertys, who extended their territory into
Inishowen from Raphoe in the 14th century, were sub-lords to the
O'Donnells. The O'Friels possessed the hereditary right of inaugurating
O'Donnell as Lords of Tirconnel. In the 14th century the O'Gormleys
were driven by the O'Donnells from their original territory in the barony
of Raphoe, and settled on the east bank of the Foyle. At the same time
the MacSweenys, descended from Scottish mercenary soldiers, the so-

31

called gallowglass, became established as a strong sept in Donegal. Another strong sept was the O'Boyles, in South Donegal, who inaugurated their chiefs at Cloghineely.

From the 10th to the 12th century the various septs of the Clan Connor, from the Laggan district in East Donegal, began to settle in the territory between the Rivers Foyle and Bann in County Derry. Their leading sept, the O'Cahans (O'Kane), overthrew the powerful sept of O'Connor of Glengiven in the Roe valley. The O'Cahans retained their ascendancy in the county until the plantation. The McCloskeys and O'Mullans were the principal septs under the O'Cahans, while the McColgans were lords in Tirkeeran barony.

In 1566 Colonel Edward Randolph sailed from Bristol, with 1,000 foot soldiers and 50 horse, for Lough Foyle to surprise from the rear the army of Shane O'Neill, Earl of Tyrone, who had risen in revolt, while the Lord Deputy of Ireland, Sir Henry Sidney, would march with his army from Dublin and attack O'Neill front on. Randolph's army landed at Derry and camped there. They expelled the inhabitants, and stored their arms in the cathedral. The soldiers were quartered in the churches and in the houses of the priests and monks. Through disease, the garrison was soon reduced to 700. Meanwhile, O'Neill mustered an army of 2,500 foot and 300 horse, and encamped 2 miles from Derry with the intention of besieging it. In a surprise ambush, O'Neill's army was defeated by the smaller English army and forced to retreat.

The garrison established in Derry, however, was short lived. On 24th April 1567 a fire broke out in the town, through an accident in the blacksmith's forge, which eventually spread to the cathedral and blew up the garrison's magazine. The only buildings left standing were St. Augustine's church, the round tower and the windmill of the monastery. The garrison now withdrew, but the priests and monks didn't return to their ruined houses. The events of 1567 marked the end of Derry as a monastic centre. For a millennium life in Derry had revolved around this monastic settlement.

By the end of the century not a trace remained of Randolph's attempt to establish an English garrison at Derry - "not a stone stood upon a stone of the city that was to be established, that it might curb the power of the Kinel-Connel and Kinel-Owen".

With Hugh O'Neill and Rory O'Donnell, Earls of Tyrone and Tyrconnel, rising against Queen Elizabeth I in 1595, the occupation of Derry was again seen as essential to contain the rebellion, by dividing and keeping in check the power of O'Neill and O'Donnell. "How often," wrote Queen Elizabeth to Lord Essex in 1599, "have you resolved us that until Lough Foyle and Ballyshannon were planted there could be no hope of doing service upon the capital rebels?"

On the 28th April 1600 an English army of 3,000 foot and 200 horse, under the command of Sir Henry Docwra, sailed into Carrickfergus to meet up with a regiment of 1,000 foot levied in Dublin. On 7th May this combined army sailed from Carrickfergus for Lough Foyle, which they entered on the 14th. They ran aground twice before landing at Culmore at 10 a.m. on the 16th May. The only resistance was a volley of shots from about 100 men, lying on shore, who quickly retired in the face of such an overwhelming force. From the top of a nearby hill their landing was observed, but not impeded, by a troop of horse and foot.

Docwra's men now set about building a fort, to garrison 200 men, against the butt end of an old dilapidated castle. Meanwhile, a company of 150 men were placed in a castle at Elagh, belonging to Sir John O'Doherty, which he had recently abandoned and begun to pull down.

On 22nd May, leaving 600 men under the command of Captain Atford to complete Culmore fort, Docwra marched his army 4 miles upstream to Derry where he found "a place in manner of an iland, comprehending within it 40 acres of ground, wherein were the ruines of an old abbay, of a bishopps house, of two churches, and, at one of the ends of it, of an old castle; the River called Loughfoyle, encompassing it all on one side, and a bogg, most comonlie wett, and not easily passable except in two or three places, dividing it from the maine land".

Docwra decided this was the place to make his main plantation. He took possession of the island, meeting no resistance. They then set about the task of building and fortifying the town in readiness for the onset of winter. They immediately dug a defensive ditch, and raised a large rampart of earth. The abbey, the cathedral and other ecclesiastical buildings were pulled down to provide building material for the new settlement. Two ships scoured the coast for building materials. Birch wood was fought for and taken from the forests in O'Cahan's land on the far side of the river; a quarry of stone and slate was opened; and cockle shells to make lime were found in the Foyle.

Docwra now erected two fortifications: one at the riverside beside the old castle, once belonging to the O'Dohertys, Lords of Inishowen and sub-Lords to the O'Donnells, which consisted of a central keep within a large bawn with three bastions, to store munitions and provisions;

another on the hill above, where the walls of the old cathedral stood, "for our future safety and retreat unto upon all occasions". Within these upper fortifications were the governor's house and housing for the garrison.

Docwra's brief was to secure Derry. His army sat out the winter of 1600 behind fortifications rather than engaging the rebels, in unfamiliar terrain, who, in any case, were attempting to avoid face-to-face confrontation. When O'Donnell saw that the English army wasn't undertaking incursions into Donegal, he assembled his forces and proceeded into Munster to plunder the territory of the Earl of Thomond. He left John Oge O'Doherty, chieftain of Inishowen, to ensure that the garrison at Derry didn't leave to plunder his territory.

With the Ulster rebellion crushed by 1603, the garrison in Derry was reduced. There was no intention of abandoning it. It was hoped Derry could now become a commercial centre. The patent rolls of James I, dated 11th July 1604, states: "the town or borough of Derrie is by reason of the natural seat and situation thereof, a place very convenient and fit to be made both a town of war and a town of merchandize."

On 19th April 1608, as a result of personal dislike and distrust between Sir George Paulett, the new governor of Derry, and Sir Cahir O'Doherty, chief of Inishowen since 1601, the city was attacked by a force under Sir Cahir's command.

On reaching the bog to the west of the city, Cahir divided his army into two parties. The first was deployed against the lower fort, where all the stores were kept. The second party climbed the hill and attacked the fort on the summit. As no sentinels watched from its watchtower, they were able to enter undetected. For two days the small garrison resisted, but they were eventually overcome and the upper and lower forts were taken and the town burnt to the ground. "The town was wholly spoiled, ransacked and fired.... the forts and church only standing, but all other buildings saving stone walls and chimneys consumed by fire."

The immediate result of this attack was the imposition of a fine on the inhabitants of Inishowen, to fund the repair of Derry's two forts, and calls for the walling of the city. Its long-term consequence, however, was an extension of the scope of the plantation of Ulster.

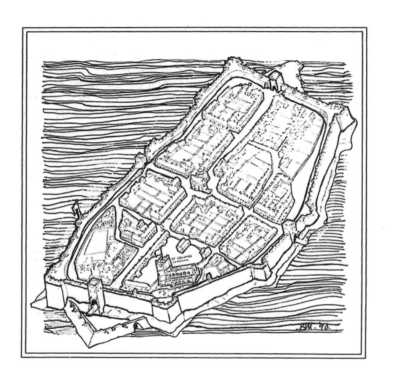

7   *The Londoners' Settlement*

In 1609 the Earl of Salisbury, Lord High Treasurer, suggested to James I a deliberate plantation of Scottish and English colonists on the forfeited estates of the O'Neills, O'Donnells and O'Dohertys. The British government was tiring of the recurring rebellions to its authority in the north of Ireland. It was now felt that the only way to deal with Ulster, described as "the most rude and unreformed part of Ireland and the seat and nest of the last great rebellion", was the creation of a new settlement strong enough to resist the native Irish.

King James I approved of this scheme, and approached the City of London to undertake the plantation of Derry and the County of Coleraine. The plantation of the other forfeited counties of Armagh, Cavan, Donegal, Fermanagh and Tyrone was to be left to private individuals who were to be granted large estates. In return, they were expected to tenant their estates with British settlers.

The City of London, with little enthusiasm for the project, turned to the 55 Livery companies for funds to meet the wishes of the king. These companies regulated and controlled their respective trades in the city. The City of London saw investment in the plantation of the Americas as more worthy of their money. The City, however, reluctantly accepted lands in Ireland. They received the County of Coleraine, together with the barony of Loughinsholin from County Tyrone; Coleraine town and its lands across the Bann from County Antrim; and Derry city and its lands across the Foyle from County Donegal. This new county was renamed Londonderry. With these additions, the plantation became more palatable to the City of London. The timber reserves of Loughinsholin, the extensive and fertile lands of the Foyle and Bann valleys and the salmon fisheries of the Foyle and the Bann at least meant the scheme had some economic potential.

On 29th March 1613 a development corporation of the City of London, called the Irish Society, was set up to manage the plantation. In 1615 the Society divided the lands of County Londonderry into 12 proportions of approximately equal value. The 55 contributors were arranged into 12 groups, each consisting of one of the principal companies and as many smaller companies as were necessary to make the total contribution of the group amount to one-twelfth of the £40,000 raised. The 12 principal companies were the Clothworkers, Drapers, Fishmongers, Goldsmiths, Grocers, Haberdashers, Ironmongers, Mercers, Merchant Taylors, Salters, Skinners and Vintners. The Merchant Taylors and Grocers, who contributed the most money, constituted a group of their own, while the Mercers had 4 associates: namely, Innholders, Cooks, Embroiderers and Masons. Each company was expected to bring in English and Scottish tenants. The focus for each proportion, to be managed by one of the 12 principal companies, was to be a village, consisting of a strong house, with a defensive bawn, and an Anglican church.

As no division could be conveniently made of the towns of Derry (renamed Londonderry) and Coleraine, or of the fisheries on the Bann and Foyle, their management was left to the Irish Society, with any profits to be divided amongst the companies.

The plan was simple: Derry in the west and Coleraine in the east were to be the focal points of the colony, while the 12 proportions were to hold, defend and develop the interior.

In 1610 Derry consisted of old ruins, a few wooden cabins and the remains of Docwra's two forts. As the River Foyle divided the O'Donnell clan of Donegal from the O'Cahans of Derry and as it stretched southward into Tyrone and the heart of O'Neill territory, it was vital to the success of the plantation to construct a strong, fortified settlement at Derry. The Londoners, however, didn't make use of the two forts they found. They demolished the upper fortifications to make way for their buildings and allowed the other to decay, so that for a number of years the town had no means to defend itself.

In 1611 a plan to fortify Derry was drawn up in which the town, extending from a frontage along the riverside and incorporating Docwra's upper and lower fortifications, would be walled on three sides, with the river fronting the fourth. This plan was not acted on.

In 1613 the Irish Society did start the construction of a city wall with the throwing up of earth ramparts and the quarrying of stone to face the ramparts. A survey carried out in 1614 noted that the work on the town wall had begun, but they were concerned that Derry still had no real defence. Towards the end of 1614 a conspiracy to launch a surprise attack on the city was unearthed and dealt with. It, however, did at least have the effect of speeding up the work of fortifying Derry.

The walls were designed by and built under the supervision of Sir Edward Doddington of Dungiven. By March 1619 when Nicholas Pynnar, the official inspector of fortifications in Ireland, visited Derry he found the city completely enclosed within a stone wall, 24 feet high by 6 feet thick. The wall was built around an earth rampart 12 feet thick and defended by 4 fortified gates, two of which, Bishop's Gate and Ferry Gate, were approached by drawbridge, with the other two, New Gate (Butcher Gate) and Water Gate (Shipquay Gate), being shut by portcullises. A ditch, 8 feet deep by 30 feet broad, ran from the Double Bastion at the west end of the city and along the south side of the walls to the river side. On the hill towards the bog no ditch was dug, as the steepness of the approach to this stretch of the walls precluded the need for one. Instead, the hill was scarped. Eleven bulwarks or bastions, on which up to 4 cannons could be placed, were spread over the wall circuit which measured 5,124 feet. All of Derry's walls could, therefore, be covered by cannon and musket fire in the event of an attempt to scale them. The approaches to Derry were further defended by the castle at Culmore, whose fortifications were strengthened between 1613 and 1618.

The plan of the new town, within the walls, was of a functional grid pattern. From the four central gates, the four principal streets met in an open area or Diamond. All other streets then met the main streets at right angles. Housing extended along both sides of the main streets, with long narrow gardens behind. Outside the walls, gardens were also laid out from the ditch to the river between Bishop's Gate and Ferry Gate.

By 1619 92 houses (including a school house, 67 feet long by 25 feet broad) had been built within the walls, housing 102 families. Many of these inhabitants were part-time farmers. On gardens allocated to them, both within and outside the city walls, crops were grown and livestock grazed. During busy times, such as sowing or harvesting, the city's streets would have been deserted as its inhabitants tended their land in the suburbs.

In 1610 Derry was in ruins, but by 1619 she was a fortified town of the continental style. Considering the London Companies' reservations on the economic potential of the plantation, this was a considerable achievement. The main worry was how a population of 102 families could defend a walled circuit nearly one mile long?

By 1622 Docwra's lower fort had been repaired to serve as a magazine. A market house, which also had a defensive role, had been built on the Diamond. Cannon could be placed on its flat roof and trained down Derry's four main streets. The old abbey, which had originally been enclosed within Docwra's upper fortification, had been repaired as a place of worship for the planters. It was, however, too small to seat them all. Between 1628 and 1633 a purpose-built Protestant church, St. Columb's Cathedral, was erected.

There were now 102 houses, made of stone and roofed with slate, within the walled city, housing 109 families, together with a few wooden cabins housing an additional 12 families. In all, 110 well-armed men could be mustered in the city, which was still insufficient to defend a city of its size.

Beyond Water Gate a quay, 300 feet long and 10 feet broad, had been made of faggots and earth. Here the river was deep enough for ships of 200 tons at low tide.

By 1640 Derry's population had risen to 500 adult males, making her the largest town in the six planted counties. At this stage the plantation of Ulster compared very favourably with that of America. Derry was very similar in size to Boston, which in 1640 had a population of 1,200.

The wisdom of constructing such a well-fortified town, the like of which had never been seen in Ireland before, was soon to be justified.

8   The Siege of Derry

In the very early years of the plantation, although there was no open revolt, the settlers were constantly harassed by gaelic swordsmen (called wood kerne) numbering some thousands, who lived in the woods which covered extensive areas of Ulster. In 1622 Thomas Phillips reported that in the Grocers' proportion robberies and murders were daily occurrences, while in the Haberdashers' proportion, which he regarded as the strongest plantation, great losses were sustained at the hands of the wood kerne. It was the rebellion of 1641, however, which proved to be the first really serious reversal the Ulster colony encountered and, not for the last time, Derry was to become the chief place of refuge for the colonists of the Ulster plantation.

In October 1641 the Irish rose in revolt under Sir Phelim O'Neill, and by 10th January 1642, according to one defender of the city, the whole of County Derry was "a prey to the rebels, and all burnt to the river side, so that the enemy braves us at the ferry, and we dare not spend a shott at him for feare of wasting our little proporcion of powder, which we keep to defend the walls when we shall be assaulted". By February 1642 some 4,000 people had fled from the countryside to the safety of Derry's walls. Many of them took ships from the quay and left for Scotland.

Derry was able to withstand the rebels as the City of London sent four ships with all kinds of provisions, while the 12 major companies sent two cannons each. Derry could withstand a siege by an ill-equipped Irish army as long as she could be supplied with provisions and munitions. Without siege battering cannon, no army could pose a military threat to Derry's fortifications.

The Irish rebellion was to become part of the wider power struggle between the royalist supporters of Charles I and the parliamentary supporters of Oliver Cromwell. By 1648 the parliamentarians controlled

Ulster. The execution of Charles I in 1649 resulted in a further rising of the native Irish in Ulster, in which all its major towns, except Derry, were captured. Derry was besieged for 20 weeks by the royalist forces under Lord Montgomery, and yet again she repulsed her attackers. By 1652 parliamentary control of Ireland was assured, and settlers started to return to the lands of the 12 London companies.

Derry resumed her growth. She was now the sixth largest town of Ireland after Dublin, Cork, Limerick, Waterford and Galway. By 1660 there were 586 adults living within the city walls and 188 outside the walls by Ferry Gate and Butcher Gate.

One November day in 1688 William III of Orange, the only legitimate Protestant grandson of Charles I of England and husband of Mary, daughter of James II, landed at Tor Bay with a Dutch fleet of 61 men-of-war and 250 transport vessels and an army of 14,000. This set off a chain of events which ended in the Siege of Derry.

James II now fled to France and the court of Louis XIV. In February 1689 William III and his wife Mary II accepted the crown of England as joint sovereigns with the approval of parliament. The deposed James now looked to Ireland as the means to win back his kingdom. In March he arrived in Ireland, and marched with his French and Irish troops towards Derry. To hold Ireland it was essential to his plans that Derry was loyal to him. However, this was not the case.

On 10th December 1688 Derry had refused to admit new garrison troops, loyal to James II, owing to rumours circulating that her citizens would be massacred. When an advance party crossed on the ferry and made their way towards Ferry Gate, 13 apprentices dropped the portcullis and locked the gate.

By 7th April 1689 James' troops had crossed the Bann. On 12th April the people and garrison of Coleraine, the second town of the plantation, evacuated to Derry, as their provisions and arms were insufficient to withstand a siege. On 13th April a detachment of James' army arrived at the Waterside, and moved on towards Strabane and the fords, further upstream, which would permit them to cross the Foyle. Robert Lundy, governor of Derry at the time, failed to secure the passes on the Finn River, and James' army crossed, with little resistance, on 15th April at Lifford, Claudy and Castlefin fords. On 17th April James arrived at St. Johnston, and sent a messenger to Derry, believing the garrison would surrender. The citizens insisted on resistance and "no surrender".

By 20th April James' forces were in position on the high ground to the west and north of the city. This high ground was well suited for bombarding the town. The island character of Derry, bounded by river on one side and swamp on the other, was of little defensive value if an enemy had specialist siege cannon. Fortunately for Derry, James had not. An encampment was also set up at Pennyburn to intercept any supplies coming from Culmore to the town.

The siege proper started on 21st April, when guns placed on high ground in Strong's orchard, on the other side of the river directly opposite Shipquay Gate, fired about 40 shots into the town, damaging the town house in the Diamond.

Derry's population had now swelled to 30,000, from its normal 2,500, owing to refugees fleeing James' army. A defensive force of 7,631 troops was mobilised. Pavements were torn up and piled up along the walls for use against the enemy. Cannons were positioned at strategic locations, two on the tower of the cathedral, four on the market house in the Diamond, one at each of the four gates and two or three on each bastion.

On 6th May the enemy advanced to the old windmill, dug a trench across the hill and down to the river, and raised a battery behind it from which they could bombard Bishop's Gate. The following day the besieged launched a two-pronged attack from Ferryquay Gate and Bishop's Gate, repulsed the besiegers from Windmill Hill, leaving 200 of them dead.

It soon became clear that, without proper siege equipment, Derry would only fall through lack of food to feed itself and arms to defend itself. On 13th June a fleet of 30 ships, commanded by Major General Kirk, entered Lough Foyle with provisions and fire-arms. By early next morning they were moored within 9 miles of the town, but for some inexplicable reason, with James' army taken by surprise, the fleet raised anchor on 15th June and sailed down the Lough. The enemy were spurred into action. They brought down cannon and raised batteries, on both sides of the river, at the outlet from Rosses Bay. There they also constructed a boom of fir planks extending across the river. (Hence the origin of the name Boom Hall.) Derry was now under effective blockade.

Attacks by the besiegers on the walls and sorties by the defenders continued. On 28th June the enemy advanced close to Butcher Gate, and set miners to work in a cellar near the gunners' bastion. In response, the besieged left by Bishop's Gate and moved towards Butcher Gate. They killed 100 of the attackers, and forced them to retreat before they could blow up and undermine this section of the wall.

As each day passed, the threat of starvation mounted. On 25th July a force of 1,600 men left by Bishop's Gate, Butcher Gate and Shipquay Gate in an attempt to capture the enemy's cattle grazing in the rear of their lines. They failed. Derry could not hold out much longer. By 28th July rations were down to 1 lb 8 ozs of horse flesh per person per day. On 29th July Major General Kirk, whose fleet was anchored in Lough Swilly, was ordered by King William to relieve Derry.

At 7 in the evening of 30th July the *Mountjoy*, with a cargo of beef, flour and biscuits and the *Phoenix*, with meal, under the protection of the frigate *Dartmouth*, approached Culmore. They came under heavy fire both from the fort at Culmore and from the cannon lining both sides of the river. The *Mountjoy*, on reaching the boom, struck it forcibly and broke it. The relief ships passed through the gap, and reached the quay at 10 p.m. With provisions replenished, the continuation of the siege was pointless. At dawn, on 1st August, James' army began their retreat. They had lost 8,000 men. Within the city 3,000 soldiers and 7,000 civilians perished through combat, hunger or disease.

Derry didn't recover quickly from the siege. At the Common Council of Londonderry Corporation on 7th July 1690 a motion was raised concerning the "ruinous state and condition of this city by reason of the late siege, and the utter inability of many of the inhabitants therein to repair their respective tenements, much less to rebuild those that are beat down by the bombs". In the same year tenants were instructed to send their rubbish and dirt to the church yard to cover the dead bodies and to fill in bomb holes.

The council minutes of 8th September 1691 acknowledged the receipt of a Queen's warrant of £1,500, paid for out of the rents of Glenarm and the Liberties of Coleraine, for the building of a new market house and for the repair of the church, free school and walls.

On 23rd May 1702 the council complained that the carriages of the guns in the city were now decayed, rendering the guns unserviceable for its defence.

It was the resilience of Derry which ensured the survival of the Ulster plantation as it attempted to establish itself under very difficult circumstances in the 17th century. Derry alone of Ulster towns managed to repulse all attacks on her, hence her title, the Maiden City. Derry's strategic significance was reflected in the fact that in 1700 she was the largest town in Ulster, with a population of some 2,000.

9 Linen Town

Through the 18th century there was a remarkable expansion of the linen industry in Ulster, largely dependent on increasing exports to Great Britain. In the period 1710 to 1770 linen exports from Ireland increased fifteen-fold. The system of work which enabled this growth evolved in the years between 1720 and 1750, and it remained in operation for nearly 100 years. It was a system that linked town and countryside together, and Derry was very much part of this system.

Prior to the 1730s the linen industry was essentially a domestic one, geared almost exclusively to supplying the family's needs as opposed to the market. A farmer would grow his own flax, scutch it, spin the yarn, weave the cloth, bleach it and, with wooden beetles, produce the finished cloth. The whole family was involved in its production; the father and sons tended the flax and wove the cloth, while the mother and daughters spun the yarn and finished the cloth.

It was the application of water-power to the bleaching and finishing processes, together with the appearance of the brown linen market from the 1720s, which marked a shift away from self-sufficiency towards producing for the market. Linen production still remained a rural activity; in fact, throughout the 18th century agriculture was largely subservient to the needs of the linen industry. Linen paid the rent, while the oats and potatoes a farmer grew and the milk he got from the one or two cows he grazed fed the family. Its production fitted in easily with the farmer's calendar, as the flax was prepared, spun and woven on the farm at the slack times of the year between seeding and harvesting.

The linchpin in this new system was the linen bleacher who purchased the weavers' webs of unbleached or brown cloth at the brown linen markets which sprang up in most Ulster towns. Derry prospered as one such centre for the sale of unbleached linen. In 1770 a purpose-built Linen Hall for the sale of brown linen was constructed inside the city walls on Rosemary Lane, later renamed Linenhall Street. It consisted of a block of small houses set round a courtyard of dimensions 147 feet by 39 feet. Prior to this the bleachers and weavers struck their deals on the street on market days.

A French visitor, named De Latocnaye, who came to the city in 1797 was impressed by the bustle of the market. He noted: "The principal trade consists in linens, of which there is a market once or twice a week. It is surprising to note the speed with which the linen merchants examine the cloth. They stand on a sort of platform with a little desk before them, while the peasants carry their webs past and stop for just a moment. The merchant looks and immediately mentions a price; if it is accepted, he marks it on the cloth, and the peasant goes to the office for payment. There is one merchant who, on every market day, buys in a single hour cloth to the value of three or four hundred pounds sterling."

In 1802 Robert Slade, secretary of the Irish Society, wrote of the linen market in Derry: "It is held twice in every week, and lasts for 2 hours only, within which short period of time I was assured linens were purchased in single webs from the manufacturers to the amount of £5,000 and upwards in ready money. These manufacturers do not reside in the city, but are dispersed in cabins around the neighbourhood, where they have each of them a few acres of land for the sake of keeping a cow and raising some potatoes and flax, and for which, by means of their looms, they are enabled to pay a heavy rent. Each man brings his web or piece of cloth and lays it before the factor, the bargain is made or rejected in a few seconds and the linen thus purchased are conveyed to the bleaching greens."

Derry acted as a focus for a thriving linen industry that extended into Counties Derry, Donegal and Tyrone. In 1816 150 weavers and 70 buyers regularly attended the linen market from this large catchment area. Derry was the natural centre for much of Counties Derry, Donegal and Tyrone, as the Foyle, Finn and Mourne river valleys of the Foyle system all converged on Derry.

In the 50 year period to 1820 County Derry became one of the major linen producing areas in Ireland, and Derry city one of its major markets. In 1820 linen to the value of £94,630 was sold in the city, making it the third biggest market, for that year, after Armagh and Lurgan. In that same year 10% of Ireland's linen exports, some 4 million yards, were shipped through the port of Derry.

Derry prospered as a linen town as long as the essentially rural-based industry depended on the town to sell the cloth it produced. In the period

1822 to 1825 Derry's long period of growth as a linen town peaked. The linen bleachers were now beginning to bypass the market.

From the 1820s bleaching was becoming concentrated in a small number of bleach greens, and these bleaching concerns started to buy direct from the weaver as opposed to the brown linen market. For example, by 1830 the Ardmore bleach green, 4 miles from Derry, extending along both sides of the River Faughan and covering 49 acres, with ten beetling machines, four wash mills and five soaping machines, powered by four water-wheels and employing up to 280 persons, bleached 500,000 yards of linen annually.

With the application of steam-power to spinning, the linen industry was to become a factory-based urban industry as opposed to a domestic rural one. Derry failed to make this transition. From 1830 onwards the linen industry was to play little part in Derry's economic health.

10   The '98 Rebellion

From the late 1770s, under the influence of the American Declaration of Independence, Ulster Protestants began to press for parliamentary reform, religious equality and economic independence. With the spread of the liberal ideas of the French Revolution, Wolfe Tone, a Protestant lawyer from Dublin, along with other like-minded Protestants, founded in Belfast in October 1791 the Society of United Irishmen. They sought an independent Ireland, free of religious and civil discrimination, and they looked to France, who was soon at war with England, for help in achieving it. The year 1798 was determined by the leaders of the United Irishmen as the right time to rise in rebellion.

In Derry the new year was heralded in with a riot among 87 prisoners on board the tender *William and James*, which was anchored in the Lough. In the early months of 1798 the talk in Derry was not of United Irishmen, but of the soldiers in the city's garrison who were intercepting farmers going to the market and stealing their provisions of meal and potatoes. On 30th March orders were issued for patrols of cavalry to be on the roads leading to the city on market days, and to arrest any soldiers more than one-quarter of a mile from the town without a pass.

There was a dramatic change on Saturday 26th May when martial law was proclaimed in the city by Brigadier General The Earl of Cavan, commander of the army in the Northern district. This was in response to a series of insurrections which broke out on 23rd May in Leinster.

On Saturday 27th May the Aberdeenshire Fencibles, previously stationed at Buncrana, arrived to strengthen Derry's garrison. The Fencibles were the home guard of the time, raised in many counties of Britain in anticipation of a Napoleonic invasion. With martial law arms of all kinds, including pikes and ammunition, had to be surrendered to the army. Furthermore, all strangers to the city had to register themselves, stating their name and business.

On Saturday 2nd June Dan McCarron of Carrigans, County Donegal, in view of the garrison troops who were paraded on the quay, received 325 lashes for administering the oath of the United Irishmen to a Private in the Tipperary Militia. The crew of four American ships (*Boston Packet, The General Washington, Sukey* and *New York*), tied up along the quay to take emigrants to the United States, witnessed the flogging. The mate form the *Sukey* was heard to utter "outrageous expressions against his Britannic majesty". He was arrested and sentenced to receive 500 lashes, but was reprieved on security of his captain, William Whitten, confining him to his vessel during her stay in the port.

On Tuesday 5th June the citizens of the city formed themselves into the Londonderry Yeoman Infantry under the command of Sir George Fitzgerald Hill, M.P. for Derry, and Andrew Ferguson.

On Thursday 7th June Ulster rose in rebellion when 6,000 men, led by Henry Joy McCraken, attacked Antrim town. In County Down Henry Munro led 7,000 men against Ballynahinch. They were totally crushed by the 13th June. Disturbances were not just confined to Down and Antrim. The Derry Journal of Tuesday 12th June reported disturbances in the county, with families from the Garvagh and Maghera areas fleeing to the city. In consequence of this alarming news a detachment of the Cambridge Cavalry, Londonderry Yeoman Cavalry, Tipperary Militia and Aberdeen Fencibles marched, from Shipquay Street at 7 p.m. on Monday 11th June, to the cheers of a large crowd, into the county to quell these disturbances.

On Tuesday 3rd July a proclamation was issued requiring all persons, except farmers carrying provisions to the army or to the market, to remain in their homes. The military now had orders to burn the houses of those who were absent. Without a licence from the General, no person would be permitted to follow the trades of gunsmith, blacksmith or whitesmith. Any offender discovered making weapons was liable to execution on his own doorstep. On Thursday 19th July John McCann was executed in front of the new jail on Bishop Street for high treason.

To accommodate troop parades for Derry's now large garrison, a new parade was built at Mall Wall, 130 yards square, extending from the Bishop's Palace to the parapet of the city wall.

Throughout 1798 Wolfe Tone had been pressing the French for assistance, but, when it came, the rebellion in Ulster had been effectively crushed. On 16th September a French fleet did set sail from Brest under the command of Commodore Bompard, consisting of one man-of-war, the *Hoche*, with 84 guns, seven frigates, with 36 to 44 guns each, and one schooner, with 18 guns. On board were 3,000 troops, artillery and a great quantity of arms for the Irish rebels. Their destination was Lough Swilly. Their instructions were to take possession of Derry and "to fortify this garrison with as much expedition as possible in order that it might serve as a rallying point for the United Irishmen, and as a strong post till they should be reinforced by fresh troops from France".

On the evening of Wednesday 10th October a British fleet under the command of Sir John Warren, consisting of three men-of-war (*Canada*, 74 guns, *Foudroyant*, 80 guns and *Robust*, 74 guns) and five frigates (*Magnanime*, 44 guns, *Amelia*, 44 guns, *Anton*, 44 guns, *Ethalion*, 38 guns and *Melampus*, 36 guns), discovered the French fleet off the Rosses, within 6 hours sail of land. They immediately gave chase which continued the whole of the next day and early into the following morning. The Derry Journal of Tuesday 16th October reported: "Early on Friday morning last, and during the entire course of that day, a most tremendous cannonading from the westward (which was heard in various parts of this neighbourhood) announced that our inveterate foe had, in again attempting to effect their atrocious plan of invasion, been encountered by the British ships which patrol the coast."

When the battle began, owing to the long chase and rough weather, both fleets were scattered. The action was a running one. The *Hoche*, the only French ship-of-the-line, fought for 3 hours with the *Robust* and *Magnanime*, until she was a dismantled wreck. She then hauled down her colours and surrendered to the *Canada*. In the very heat of the fight a Scottish seaman on board the *Canada*, seeing that the ship's colours were shot away, ran aloft and nailed the colours to the mast. Out of her complement of 1,300 men, including troops, the *Hoche* had 200 killed or wounded.

When the *Hoche* surrendered the rest of the French fleet took flight. Pursuit was given. The *Anton*, which lost her mizzen-mast in the chase, engaged five of the enemy's ships and had three on her at once for a long space of time. Soon after the chase began three of the French frigates surrendered and were taken possession off. Another was captured in Donegal Bay by the *Melampus*. The chase continued for 36 hours, but the other French ships evaded capture by lightening themselves by throwing overboard their chests, spare masts, stores of every kind and even their lifeboats.

The British fleet now returned to Lough Swilly. On 17th October one of the frigates which had escaped Sir John Warren's fleet was "left almost a total wreck" by the Royal Navy frigate, *Mermaid*, 40 miles west of Tory Island.

On Monday 22nd October Sir John Warren, commander of the squadron, arrived in Derry to pay a visit to the Custom House. The following day he was entertained at Nelsons by the Londonderry Yeoman Cavalry.

It was Wednesday 31st October, owing to the stormy weather, before the *Hoche* could be towed into Lough Swilly, and it was Saturday 3rd November before the wind fell enough to allow 500 of the prisoners to be landed. They were escorted to the jail in Derry by a party of the Breadalbane and Somersetshire Fencibles. "Some of them are well looking, others wretched in their appearance. They are coarsely and variously clothed, the uniform most distinguishable is blue, fac'd with white. They seemed delighted by getting on shore, and many of them declared they were happy in being made prisoners, having been forced into the service and expecting to be led to certain death."

On Monday 5th November, after spending two nights in the jail on Bishop Street, 200 of the prisoners, under a strong escort, left for Lifford. On the 11th and 12th the remaining prisoners were sent off, in detachments, to Newry for shipment to England. Prisoners held on board ship in Lough Swilly were shipped direct to Liverpool from there on the 6th November.

"The only Irishman as yet discovered among the prisoners is the celebrated Theobald Wolfe Tone.... On landing he was immediately recognised by many of his college and bar acquaintances." On landing at Buncrana he was brought to the castle where Lord Cavan resided. From there he was escorted to Derry gaol by Lord Cavan's Aid-de-Camp, Captain Chester. On his arrival there on Saturday 3rd November he was put in irons. Two days later, on Monday 5th November, Tone was escorted to Dublin to face trial as a traitor. On 8th November, sitting in a carriage and dressed in the uniform of a French Colonel, Tone entered Dublin. He was tried on the 10th, and sentenced to be executed on the 12th. He, however, cut his own throat, eventually dying on the 19th November.

William Pitt, the Prime Minister, was now convinced that a union of Ireland and Great Britain was essential if further rebellion was to be avoided. An Act of Union was passed, and it came into effect on 1st January 1801.

11   *Georgian Elegance*

Visitors to the city in August 1829, drawn in by the big social occasions of the Londonderry Races and the Summer Assizes, would have been impressed with what they saw, especially if they had any knowledge of the city of 30 years before.

Inside the city walls Derry's architecture was beginning to reflect her growing prosperity. The main entrances to the city had been rebuilt: Bishop's Gate, in 1789, as a triumphal arch, while Shipquay Gate, between 1805 and 1808, was widened and finished with sandstone facing. In the Diamond stood Corporation Hall, largely rebuilt in 1823, capped by a small square tower with a cupola. Through its circular entrance, facing Bishop Street, access was gained to the upper floor, where the city council met, and to the Assembly Hall where public dinners and balls were held.

Shipquay Street rose steeply with a succession of typical Georgian houses stepping up the hill: graceful, red-bricked buildings of three or four storeys, with entrances (owing to the street's steepness) by way of steps and balconies bounded with metal railings. The steep-pitched roofs were slated and topped with red-brick chimney stacks on which perched six, seven or even eight chimney pots. The simplicity of design, the symmetry of the windows, only broken on the ground floor with decorative, round-headed doorways, all made for a distinctive street which was further enhanced by its setting. Through the gate and over the top of the city's walls the masts of sailing ships, tied along the quay, were clearly visible. Across the river an enticing piece of undulating wooded parkland could be seen and, within its grounds, St. Columb's House, a large two-storey stuccoed house. This was the home and demesne of Sir George Fitzgerald Hill, M.P. for the city and Clerk of the Race Course.

Likewise Bishop Street, another major commercial street, was very

Georgian in character. Above the roof level of the rather stately three-storey, red-brick houses could be seen the spire of St. Columb's Cathedral. By the gate stood the new court house which had been completed between 1813 and 1817. This was the finest building in the city, modelled in the style of a classical Greek temple with a portico. Opposite it, and dating from 1753, was a three-storey, red-brick building with two projecting wings. This was the Bishop's Palace. Through the gate and just outside the walls was the recently refurbished jail. Between 1819 and 1824 turrets were added to the fronting two-storey block, built in 1791, and a circular cell block was added at the rear.

The city walls were now a favourite place on which to walk. Grand Parade, created when the Bishop's Palace was temporarily converted into an army barracks between 1798 and 1803, was especially popular as it led to the Royal Bastion where the year before (i.e. 1828) Walker's monument had been erected. On top of an 81 feet column of Portland stone, ascended by a spiral staircase of 110 steps, stood a 9 feet statue of Governor Walker, his right hand clutching a bible and in his left a sword pointing towards the river and to the ships which relieved Derry in 1689.

From the city walls, the expansion which was beginning to occur to the north could be seen. Clearly visible, in its own grounds of some 12 acres, could be seen the Lunatic Asylum which was completed that year (i.e. 1829). It was a substantial building, its most distinctive feature being a clock tower, over the centre of the building, with an octagonal cupola. Beyond the asylum stood Foyle College, a three-storey, five-bay central block, flanked by two-storey, single-bay blocks, which took in its first pupils in 1814.

William Street, Rossville Street and Abbey Street had been recently reclaimed, and housing now extended along these streets. The land between the rear of the houses on William Street and the grounds of the asylum were meadow. Goats and donkeys grazed on the grass and brambles here. However, this was soon to change. From the 1830s houses for the merchant and professional classes appeared here along Strand Road, and along a criss-cross of streets running uphill from it. By 1835 Sackville Street, Great James Street and Little James Street had been laid out, and were soon built on with terraces of Georgian style, two-bay, three-storey, red-brick buildings. A Presbyterian meeting house, fronted by four ionic columns, opened in 1837, half-way up Great James Street. By 1847 the remaining slob and meadow ground between Great James Street and the asylum had been laid out in neat rectangular blocks with Patrick Street, Clarendon Street and Asylum Road running uphill, and Edward Street, Queen Street and Princes Street running across the hill at right angles. Terraces of fine Georgian houses soon followed, and another Presbyterian church was opened in 1847 at the corner of Patrick Street and Strand Road. Georgian improvements were not just confined to architecture. Municipal services also benefited. Water was now brought to the city through a series of pipes from a reservoir in the Waterside, 2 miles away. The city no longer had to rely on water-pumps within the city and wells outside it for her water supply. With the erection of a gasworks in Foyle Street in 1829 the city was now well lit by coal gas, whereas before it had been dimly lit with oil lamps. A night watch had been established, to ensure among other things that the bridge didn't go on fire. This was necessary as Derry's first bridge, built in 1790, was made of wood. Fire engines were operational, if need be, 24 hours a day. The Assizes were now held in the purpose-built court house as opposed to the town hall. The streets were maintained in good order. Those contracted by the Grand Jury to undertake the repair of Derry's roads were, in 1838, paying 2 shillings 9 pence per ton of stones broken in Derry jail by her inmates.

It was also the age of charitable endowments. In 1829 John Gwyn, a linen merchant of the city, died and bequeathed £40,000 for the feeding, clothing and education of the poorest male children in the area. John Gwyn had been orphaned at an early age. The cholera epidemic of 1832 left so many destitute children in the city that the City Hotel in Shipquay Street was rented to house them until a new school could be built behind the city infirmary. Gwyn's Institute, a two-storey building with three projecting wings and finished in sandstone and set in 10 acres of ground, was opened in 1840.

Georgian elegance was even reflected in the new barracks for the city's garrison which could accommodate 600 men. In 1839, between the river and the Limavady Road, a barracks was laid out. Regular blocks of three-storey buildings were set around three sides of a parade ground, with the west side, facing across the Foyle towards the city, left open.

The big social events of the year in Derry at this time were the Races and the Assizes. From Monday 3rd August to Thursday 6th August 1829 there was a full horse-racing programme at the race course at Ballyarnet: on Monday the 100 guineas King's Plate and the Antrim Hunt Stakes; on Tuesday the Ulster Hunters' Stakes, confined to horses used in hunting; on Wednesday the Farmers' Stakes for horses belonging to farmers; on Thursday a Hack's Race with 10 sovereigns prize money. When the meeting opened on the Monday there were no fewer than 10,000 spectators. The Stewards reported, however, a reduction in the number of gentry attending and, as a consequence, a falling off in funds to attract the best horses. It was the patronage of the gentry, by sponsoring the various plates and stakes, which had enabled the Derry Races to remain as one of the premier race meets since the late 18th century.

The theatre, at the junction of Artillery Lane and London Street, which had opened in 1789, was very fashionable during Race Week. As it was the gentry and officers from the garrison who made up the audiences, and filled its boxes as well as the seats in the pit and gallery, performances tended to be infrequent outside the big events on the social calendar. This year was no exception. The theatre re-opened during Race Week for six evening performances, through to Saturday 8th August, by Miss Jarman of the Theatre Royal, Covent Garden in London.

The Race Week had been preceded by a pleasure excursion on Wednesday evening, 29th July, on the paddle-steamer *Foyle* to the islands of Staffa and Iona in the Hebrides. In favourable weather the sight-seeing party returned to Derry, after a 36 hour voyage, at 5 a.m. on Friday. On Saturday 1st August a boat race from Culmore to Quigley's Point and back, which originated in a bet between two gentlemen of the city, attracted a large crowd of well-to-do spectators.

The Summer Assizes resulted in a further round of social events. Indeed, Sir George Hill, Clerk of the Race Course, had the power to postpone the race meeting for a few days if it clashed with the Assizes. In 1829 the Summer Assizes for the city and county of Londonderry were to commence on Friday 21st August at the court house in Bishop Street. On Thursday afternoon Judge Vandeleur and Baron Pennefather arrived in Derry from Lifford where the Donegal Assizes had been held. That Friday at 10 a.m. the 23 members of the Grand Jury for the county (usually landlords or their agents) were sworn in. They then immediately proceeded to deal with any civil and criminal business.

The evenings were reserved for big social gatherings. The theatre re-opened with a performance of "The Rivals" on the Friday night which "attracted a most fashionable and crowded audience". On Monday 24th August the Assizes Ball was held at the Corporation Hall, at which upwards of 200 people attended. At 2 a.m. they sat down to supper, with dancing continuing till 5 in the morning. The Derry Journal reported: "We have not witnessed for a long time so great a display of beauty and fashion."

In 1829 the gentry still found Derry a fashionable place to visit during Race Week and Assizes Week, while at the same time, a growing merchant class were beginning to live in rather attractive town houses, both within the walls and in the suburbs to the north. The result: a vibrant, attractive city.

12   *A Busy Port*

If you had walked along Derry's quay, which then stretched from the wooden bridge at Bridge Street to the slip (for dry-docking ships) at Lower Clarendon Street, during the week ending Monday 2nd June 1834 you would have come across dock-hands loading and unloading ships, bumped into passengers awaiting embarkation and seen many wooden sailing vessels, both large and small, and a few wooden paddle-steamers docked along the quay.

In that week five ships with a full complement of emigrants sailed from the port: the *Ontario*, which had been delayed due to unfavourable winds, for New York; the 800 ton *Henry Gratton*, the 800 ton *Macedonia* and the American-owned *Cyrus Butler* (whose agent in the city, William McCorkell, was later to become one of the biggest ship-owners in Derry) for Philadelphia; and the brig *Mary Cumming*, copper-fastened for extra protection, for Quebec. A further six ships, contracted by Derry merchants, arrived from Liverpool to pick up passengers: the 1,000 ton *Senator* for New York; the *Ceylon* and *John Bouwer* for Philadelphia; the *Robert Burns* and the *Ranger*, whose passengers were advised to board by Thursday 5th June as she was to sail the first fair wind, for St. John, New Brunswick; and the *Irton* for Quebec.

Passengers intending to board the *Ceylon* were advised by James Corscaden, the agent: "Those holding orders from America, will please have them returned immediately and their names entered." Derry's emigrant trade depended to a large extent on people in the U.S. and Canada paying the fare to bring out family and friends.

Three other ships were daily expected to pick up passengers: the *Snowden* and *Ellen Gordon* for St. John, and the *Carouge* for Philadelphia.

Derry was thriving as an emigration port, and she had been for the one hundred years prior to 1834. In the age of sail Derry possessed an ideal situation. She stood at the head of a virtually land-locked Lough Foyle, 24 miles long and only 2 miles wide at its head. The Lough was sheltered from the prevailing westerly winds by the Inishowen peninsula, thus making it, in the age of sail, a harbour of refuge, accessible and safe in all weather. She was, therefore, able to benefit from the widespread emigration of Ulster people to North America from the early 1700s.

In the years 1771 and 1772 a slump in the linen trade was reflected in an increase in emigration, when it is estimated 17,150 left through the five principal ports of the north of Ireland on 61 ships. Twenty-two of these, of which 16 were destined for Philadelphia, carrying 6,300 emigrants or 36% of the total, left from Derry. Belfast, the next largest, carried 4,200 emigrants or 26% of the total.

Derry's importance as an emigration port increased throughout the 19th century. It was a profitable trade. Merchants in Derry soon became ship-owners as opposed to agents for American and British companies. An outward cargo of emigrants, a homeward cargo of timber or grain, together with two voyages per year, one in spring and one in the autumn, ensured a sizeable profit. By 1833 seven merchants in the city owned fifteen vessels, all engaged in the North American trade.

Two local companies, J & J Cooke and William McCorkell & Co, by the 1850s had built up sizeable shipping fleets. Between 1847 and 1867 J & J Cooke carried 21,000 passengers to North America. In this period the firm bought nine ships specifically for the emigration trade. Emigrants carried by them came from Enniskillen in the south to Malin in the north, and from Donegal town in the west to Ballymoney in the east.

In the mid-1860s William McCorkell & Co had five ships plying between Derry and New York and Philadelphia: the *Mohongo*, *Minnehaha*, *Stadacona*, *Village Belle* and *Lady Emily Peel*. The *Minnehaha*, known in New York as "the green yacht from Derry", maintained a service of two voyages per year to New York throughout the American Civil War.

From the 1870s steam took over from sail on the transatlantic routes. Right down to 1939 would-be emigrants were carried down the River Foyle in paddle-tenders from Queen's Quay in the heart of the city to connect with the steamships of the Anchor and Allan Lines that anchored, 18 miles downstream, at Moville.

Going back to our walk down the quay in June 1834, we would have found many small sailing vessels, all employed in the coasting trade with Britain. Five ships with cargoes of coal, two from Irvine, one from

Glasgow, one from Ayr and one from Workington, were being unloaded on the quay. This coal was earmarked for Derry's growing industrial base, such as the three recently opened steam grain mills, along the quayside, and the three distilleries at Pennyburn, Abbey Street and Waterside, as well as for domestic heating. In addition to these coal boats, the *Mary Ann* arrived from Bowmore, Isle of Islay with a cargo of potatoes, the *Amity* from Beaumaris in Anglesey with slates and the *Harriet* from Liverpool with general cargo. A further four boats were being loaded with oats, three destined for Glasgow and one for Liverpool. Another boat sailed to Campbelltown with a cargo of beer. All these sailing ships were small in size with the crew, in many cases, consisting of a master, two men and a boy.

A relatively new addition, at this time, to Derry's coasting trade were the paddle-steamers operating to a timetable to both Liverpool and Glasgow. Funnels, from which smoke belched out, could now be seen alongside the masts of the sailing ships. It was not unknown at this time for adverse weather conditions to detain sailing ships, especially the heavy-laden ones, for up to 6 weeks. In 1829 with the purchase of its first steamer, the 136 ton *Foyle*, Derry merchants could offer regular sailings. This benefited trade immensely. More steamers were bought, and by 1834 the *Foyle* and *Londonderry* sailed to Glasgow every week, the former on a Friday and the latter on a Tuesday, and the *Robert Napier* and *Queen Adelaide* sailed for Liverpool weekly, the former on a Saturday and the latter on a Wednesday. The 139 mile journey to Glasgow, with stops at Moville, Portrush, Giant's Causeway, Campbelltown and Greenock, took 22 hours, while the 215 mile crossing to Liverpool took 28 hours. These steamships carried linen, provisions, livestock and passengers from Derry. The return cargo consisted of luxury items such as tobacco, whisky, sugar and tea. Without steam navigation the markets of Liverpool and Glasgow were largely inaccessible to the farmers of Derry, Donegal and Tyrone. Until the steamship brought efficient and reliable communications between Britain and Derry the export of grain and livestock was not feasible. Before the steamboat eggs could not be exported, yet by 1834 eggs to the value of £70,000 were shipped to Britain. The steamship afforded a ready and constant outlet for farm produce - a farmer with access to Derry port could now compete on equal terms with those English and Scottish farmers living 60 miles from Liverpool and Glasgow respectively.

With our walk along the quay completed, we couldn't help but be impressed with the sights, sounds and smells of a busy port. We would leave with the vision of large wooden sailing vessels, destined for the transatlantic routes, tied up alongside the small sailing ships and paddle-steamers of the coasting trade; of cargoes of coal, potatoes and slate, unloaded and stacked on the dockside and of gangs of dockers humping bags of oats and barrels of beer up gangways into ships' holds; of reluctant livestock being herded onto the steamships, watched by the many labourers who were waiting to board the same ships for harvest work on the mainland; of the crowds of people, gathered by the larger sailing vessels, to see off friends and relatives who were emigrating to a new life in America; of small traders selling straw, for bedding, and bags of biscuits to boarding emigrants; of the industries, crafts, shops and services (such as boarding-houses, blockmakers, coopers, rope-makers, ship-brokers and ship-chandlers) by the quayside to serve the needs of a booming port. We would probably remark on the variety of English-speaking accents, as the voices of Derry crew members mingled with English, Scottish, Welsh and American voices.

By 1834 the Derry-owned sailing fleet of 41 ships, including 15 involved in the North American emigrant trade, employed a crew of 344 men. Most of these men were locals. In Rossville Street alone there lived seven master mariners. In the same year, i.e. 1834, 649 vessels entered the port of Derry, while 646 ships departed from it. More local men were employed in the loading and unloading of these ships. It is no coincidence that the height of Derry's prosperity coincided with a thriving port.

13   Industrial Boom

In 1821 Derry was the twelfth largest town in Ireland, by 1911 she was the fourth. In 1821 Derry was only twice as big as her rivals, Strabane and Coleraine, and four times the size of Letterkenny. By 1911 she was five times as big as Coleraine, eight times the size of Strabane and eighteen times the size of Letterkenny.

In 1821, with a burgeoning coasting trade in linen and provisions to Britain, a growing emigration trade to North America and a prosperous linen industry, Derry was a small but vigorous town of 9,313 souls. Apart from Belfast, whose population increased ten-fold, no other town of significance in Ireland had anywhere near the rate of growth of Derry. In fact, of the eighteen major Irish towns in 1821 with a population of over 8,000 eleven had declined in size by 1911. Seven did increase in size, but only two, Belfast and Derry, actually more than doubled in size.

How does one account for this growth? In the 19th century expansion was the exception rather than the norm within Ireland. Yet during that time Derry stamped her dominance over her local rivals, and emerged as an important urban centre within Ireland. The answer lies in Derry experiencing an Industrial Revolution. From the 1830s a succession of entrepreneurs, both local-born and from Britain, especially Scotland, appeared on the scene and established new industries or expanded old ones. These men put Derry at the forefront of technology in the 19th century. They identified new markets, introduced new ideas and new methods of work organisation. In shirt-making, shipbuilding and distilling Derry was to compete successfully with the rest of the world.

The shirt industry grew, in the space of 50 years, from virtually nothing to become the principal seat of the shirt industry in the UK and an exporter to all over the world. It was the enterprise of one man, namely William Scott, which laid the foundations of this new industry.

At the age of 66 William Scott, a linen-weaver from Ballougry, outside the city, saw that there was a growing demand in the cities of Britain for cotton shirts with embroidered fronts. In 1831 he got his wife and daughters to make a few shirts which he took with him on the steamer to Glasgow. He returned with the shirts sold and orders for more. By 1840 he had set up an "outworker system" whereby, at stations spread throughout Counties Derry, Donegal and Tyrone, local girls, long skilled in working with linen, were provided with the material, to make up shirts in their own homes, from his factory at Bennett's Lane where the weavers, cutters, examiners and packers were based. By 1850 this business had grown to such an extent that the wage bill of William Scott & Son of £500 per week was one of the highest in the city.

In the 1850s Scott's initial success attracted a number of Scottish businessmen who brought with them new methods of factory organisation and new technology in the form of the sewing machine. William Tillie arrived in Derry from Glasgow in 1850, and with his partner, John Henderson, erected, in 1857, a five-storey building, covering nearly one acre of land on Foyle Road, with 19,000 square feet of factory space. At that time this shirt factory was the largest of its kind in the world. The sewing machines and cutting machines were all driven by steam-power. By 1890 Tillie and Henderson employed 1,500 hands in their factory, and provided work for 3,000 outworkers in Counties Derry, Donegal and Tyrone. They had wholesale warehouses in London and Glasgow and they exported overseas to Australia, South Africa, North and South America and the West Indies.

Other factories followed. Peter McIntyre, from Paisley, and Adam Hogg, from Melrose, opened the City Factory in Queen Street in 1864. In 1876 the London firm of Welch Margetson moved into new premises in Carlisle Road, and they were soon employing 1,000 together with 3,000 outworkers.

So great was the demand for Derry-made shirts from Glasgow and London that the number of shirt factories in the city increased from 5 in the 1850s to 44 by 1926. At its peak in the mid 1920s the Derry shirt industry employed 8,000 and provided work for an additional 10,000 outworkers. Confidence in the shirt industry was reflected in the massive red-brick factories that were built. When David Hogg and Charles Mitchell opened their five-storey factory in Great James Street in 1898 a specially chartered steamer was hired to bring over guests from England.

The beginnings of a shipbuilding industry in Derry can be assigned to 1830 when Pitt Skipton, of Beech Hill near the city, and John Henderson, a Dungiven linen-bleacher, reclaimed slob land to the north of the Shipquay and erected a slip dock for the repair of vessels, 300 tons in size. In 1835 they employed Captain William Coppin (who, though still only 30, had designed and built sailing vessels in Canada for Derry merchants, captained sailing vessels on the West Indian trade route and commanded the Derry-to-Liverpool steamer) to build a West Indian sugar-trader for the Derry firm Pitt & Co. The resulting 180 ton *Sir Robert Alexander Ferguson*, built of Irish oak from the nearby forests of Walworth and Learmount, was a significant landmark. It marked a shift away from total reliance on repair work to the construction of ships. More importantly, it began Captain Coppin's 35-year association with the city.

In 1839 William Coppin bought the yard of Pitt Skipton & Co, and by 1840 he was employing 500 men in building new vessels, ship repairs and salvage work. His greatest achievement was on the 23rd July 1842, when 20,000 persons, who had gathered since 8 a.m., watched the launch of his three-masted, screw-propelled, 274 feet long, 1,750 ton, 360 horsepower steamship, *The Great Northern*. The Illustrated London News, on witnessing its arrival in the East India Docks, regarded it as "a remarkable monument of marine architecture".

In creativity and inventiveness Coppin was far ahead of his competitors. This was his downfall because he could find no buyer for such a new and unproven design. In 1850 he had to sell the ship for scrap, and from then until the yard closed in 1870 Coppin concentrated on repair and salvage work.

In 1882 shipbuilding returned to Derry when local man Charles Bigger set up the Foyle Shipyard at a new site at Pennyburn. He specialised in constructing large steel-hulled sailing ships, and before its closure in 1892 the yard built 26 sailing ships, including five for local merchant, William Mitchell, and 7 steamers. Shipbuilding resumed again from 1899 to 1904. In 1912 the yard was re-equipped and four new berths, up to 1,000 feet in length, were constructed. During the First World War the yard was working flat out, 24 hours a day, to replace allied shipping losses. By 1918 the workforce totalled 2,000 men. The yard continued to expand after the war, and the workforce grew to 2,600 in the early years of the 1920s, with a weekly wage bill of £7,000. Derry's future as a major shipbuilding centre seemed secure; it had the third largest output in all Ireland. Yet in 1924 the yard closed for the last time, owing to a deepening world depression.

Although never a permanent fixture, shipbuilding was a very significant employer in the city. As a major male employer it acted as a counterbalance to the predominantly female workforce of Derry's shirt industry. It resulted in the attraction of a small Scottish community to the city when Scottish shipwrights, platers, boilermakers, caulkers and drillers came to live in streets such as Glasgow Terrace and Argyle Terrace.

By 1830 Derry had a small whiskey-distilling industry with distilleries at Pennyburn, Waterside and Abbey Street producing over 200,000 gallons of whiskey annually between them. In 1839 David Watt, the son of Andrew Alexander Watt, a leading merchant in the city, acquired full ownership of the Abbey Street distillery, and began the expansion that was to make Watt's distillery one of the largest in the UK. When Aeneas Coffey invented the patent-still, the Abbey Street distillery was one of the first to have it installed, with Mr Coffey personally supervising its installation in 1833. The grain whiskey produced had a milder flavour to the malt whiskey produced in pot-stills at Pennyburn.

In 1870 David Watt took over the Waterside distillery from the Mehan family. By 1887 the two Coffey patent-stills, seven storeys high, within the 8 acre Abbey Street complex, produced 1,260,000 gallons of grain whiskey annually and employed some 200 men, while its Waterside distillery produced 200,000 gallons of malt whiskey. Like shipbuilding, the end for Watts, and its "Old Tyrconnel" grain whiskey and "Old Inishowen" malt whiskey, came with the depression and the resultant contracting market in the inter-war years.

In 1900 Derry was an old-established manufacturing centre where growth seemed assured. In the three decades to 1911 the population had doubled. It was a place of opportunity offering good employment prospects. Her growing industries attracted workers and families from outside the city. For example, of 31 households living in Argyle Terrace in 1901, 19 of them had origins outside the county; 10 of the heads of household were born in Scotland, while 8 had come from County Donegal to live in this one street. The shipyard and bakery were the major employers with 11 of these households depending on them; 6 on the shipyard and 5 on the bakery. Not only did the head of household find employment in Derry, but so too did the rest of the family. For example, in one family group on Argyle Terrace the father, born in Scotland, worked as a baker, while the 25 year old daughter found employment as an examiner in a shirt factory, the 18 year old son as an apprentice baker and the 16 year old son as a rivet boy in the shipyard.

In 1900 Derry seemed capable of sustaining economic growth. Yet by the 1930s the shipbuilding and distilling industries had ceased, while the shirt industry contracted in the face of cheap imports from Europe.

14   *The Troubles*

With the First World War over, a crisis was looming in Ireland. The General Election of 1918 returned 73 Sinn Fein MPs who refused to take their seats at Westminster. On 21st January 1919 they met together at Dublin Mansion House, and formed their own assembly, Dail Eireann. Independence was declared. Through 1919 clashes between British Crown forces and Republicans became more frequent and serious, as guerrilla warfare against the Royal Irish Constabulary was stepped up.

In Derry this turmoil was restricted to sporadic rioting. In the early hours of Saturday morning, 16th August, rioters smashed and looted their way through Ferryquay Street and Butcher Street. More trouble was expected that evening, so troops were kept in readiness in the court house on Bishop Street. After midnight, however, with everything quiet, the military returned to their barracks in the Waterside.

In 1920, however, events in Derry were to take a dramatic turn for the worse. The year started off with municipal elections. The result was going to be the closest ever, as this was to be Derry's first ever election under the proportional representation system. It was billed as "the greatest fight which had been waged in the history of Derry for control of civic affairs". The result: the Nationalists won 21 seats, the Unionists 19. It was the first time that the Nationalists had secured a majority on the city council. On 2nd February the Derry Journal reported: "For the first time at least since the reign of King James II a Catholic again holds the office of Mayor of Derry." The new Mayor was a solicitor, Hugh C O'Doherty. The Journal went on to say: "A Hindu quack doctor once stood a fair chance of being elected, but the upholders of civil and religious liberty always drew the line at a papist."

The situation was becoming tense. Unionists, accustomed to ruling for so long, no doubt resented Nationalist control of the city's affairs. More critically, there were many aimless, unemployed ex-soldiers in Derry, both Nationalist and Unionist, with rifles in their possession, now that the war was over.

On Wednesday 14th April a large crowd, awaiting the arrival of a Sinn Fein prisoner at the Great Northern Railway station on Foyle Street, clashed with the army and police escort due to take the prisoner to the jail on Bishop Street. The rioters were dispersed along Foyle Street and up Bridge Street. The army had to force a passage for the lorry carrying the prisoner to the jail. Later a crowd of Republican sympathisers gathered outside the jail, to be joined by a Unionist crowd from Fountain Street. A riot soon started, with the two sides pelting each other over the heads of the police who, with bayonets fixed, were attempting to separate them.

The following Saturday, 17th April, a fierce riot originated with an attack by a gang of youths on two soldiers at the top of Bridge Street. The police were fired at as they pushed the crowd down Carlisle Road. Two hundred soldiers of the Dorset Regiment were called in to reinforce the police who were now being attacked in Ferryquay Street. At bayonet point the rioters were driven through the Diamond and dispersed up Bishop Street and down Shipquay Street. At 10.15 p.m. a fight broke out between Unionists congregated at the foot of Fountain Street and Republican sympathisers in the Bridge Street area. From Bridge Street came the call: "Send down bullets, not bricks." The police charged down Ferryquay Street, reformed, then charged, with bayonets fixed, down Bridge Street and cleared it. Simultaneously, a cordon of military was drawn along Carlisle Road, at the foot of Fountain Street, and the crowd retired for the night lustily singing "God save the King".

At this point the Lecky Road Police Barracks came under attack. The windows were riddled with bullets, and an attempt was made to force the door with huge boulders. From behind sandbagged windows the garrison of 6 police replied with revolver fire. Police reinforcements and 50 soldiers, heading down Fahan Street to relieve the barracks, were fired at. They got through, however, and dispersed the crowd that had been attacking the barracks for over 30 minutes. By 2 a.m. all was quiet, and the police and soldiers were withdrawn.

The next evening, Sunday 18th April, rioting again erupted, and shots were fired from the foot of Wapping Lane in the direction of the bridge. It was so severe that pedestrians couldn't cross the bridge and had to stay the night where they were.

On Monday the Catholic clergy moved about the streets to a late hour, in an attempt to prevent a recurrence of the previous two nights rioting, persuading people to go home. The night passed quietly.

Sporadic trouble flared over the next four or five weeks. On Sunday 13th June a relatively minor incident led to a spiralling of events and incidents that soon got out of control. On that morning a Sinn Fein excursion party returning to Derry in a char-a-banc, singing "the Soldiers Song", was ambushed at Prehen wood. Shots were exchanged, but there were no injuries. On 18th June the Derry Journal reported that in Prehen wood up to 50 unemployed Unionist ex-soldiers were gathering each day and threatening to kill any Sinn Feiner found in the area. On Friday 18th June a riot broke out between Catholics and Protestants in the Waterside, and it was later seen as the spark which ignited the "powder-keg".

Around 8 p.m. on Saturday 19th June a drunken squabble took place outside Bishop's Gate, directly opposite Long Tower Street. By 9 p.m. it had developed into a violent riot. Then a number of Unionists, armed with rifles and revolvers, opened fire on the Long Tower from the city walls and from the Unionist strongholds of Fountain Street and Albert Street. From Long Tower Street Nationalists replied with revolver shots. Keeping up rapid fire, the Unionists were able to gradually work their way down Bishop Street, forcing the Nationalist group, who had rushed up Shipquay Street to the Diamond, to retreat along Butcher Street and down Shipquay Street. The Unionists took possession of the Diamond at 10 p.m., and posted armed men at the head of Shipquay Street and Butcher Street, from which they kept up a continuous fire. When a strong detachment of the Dorset Regiment arrived at 11 p.m. the armed Unionists withdrew to Fountain Street. Meanwhile, for three hours the Lecky Road Police Barracks had been subjected to intermittent rifle fire. The night left five dead and seventeen wounded.

On Monday evening 21st June masked parties of Unionists, carrying rifles with fixed bayonets, took possession of Carlisle Square. In doing so they commanded entry to the city over the bridge. From Carlisle Road they exchanged fire with Nationalists in Bridge Street. Nationalists, armed with service rifles, discharged a volley of shots into the Unionist area from Butcher Street.

On Tuesday 22nd June a telegram was sent to the Prime Minster requesting the government to proclaim martial law and to send sufficient troops to enforce it. The troops garrisoned in Derry were unable to quell the situation. Armed Unionists in the Waterside were keeping Carlisle Bridge under fire. All shops were closed and streets deserted.

On Wednesday 23rd June two companies of the Norfolk Regiment arrived by special train at the Great Northern Railway Station; by the evening they were posted at the Diamond, searching all pedestrians. A destroyer arrived in the Foyle, and stationed itself opposite the Guildhall, its searchlight playing on the city to locate snipers. The Unionists still controlled Carlisle Bridge and the entrance to the city. The army were now firing on the snipers, and they rounded up a number of Unionists in the Waterside who had been firing towards Bridge Street.

On Thursday 24th June a conference was held between the army officers of the city's garrison and the captain of the destroyer. A curfew was announced, and all merchants were requested to reopen their business premises.

On Saturday 26th June business resumed, as did sailings of the Glasgow steamer. Derry was now quiet, with the military in control. The six day "civil war" had left 23 dead and many wounded.

On 6th December 1921, with a treaty signed between Britain and Ireland, the partitioning of Ireland by the Government of Ireland Act of November 1920, came into effect. Derry, controlled by a Nationalist council, was now part of Northern Ireland. Many Nationalists, however, felt it was only a matter of time before it would be part of the Free State, as the treaty allowed for boundary modifications to take account of local Catholic majorities. With a Nationalist population of 22,923 out of 40,780, i.e. a majority of 56%, it was expected Derry could opt out of Northern Ireland.

In any case, many Nationalists felt that the Unionists in the city were not in favour of partition; their economic interest would see to that, as the wholesale trade of the city was dependent on County Donegal. Protestant merchants had built up successful businesses out of their trade with Donegal. Much of the cross-channel goods imported through Derry quay found their way through Derry's substantial retail and wholesale network into Donegal. It was carried there by railways, reaching north to Carndonagh and west to Burtonport, which Derry merchants had helped to build up and fund.

On 1st February 1922 the Mayor formally proposed: "This council and the majority of the citizens are greatly concerned lest the country of the city of Derry should be cut off from the Free State, with which its interests are indissolubly bound up."

It was perhaps the feeling that Derry would soon be part of the Free State which accounts for no repetition of the violence of April and June 1920.

By June 1922 events were heading towards a civil war in the Free State between the new government and the anti-treaty Republicans, while

Belfast reeled under the backlash of Protestant anger. Derry remained remarkably quiet, only rail services into Donegal being suspended for a while because of ambushes, across the border, by the anti-treaty Irregulars.

The civil war which dragged on to May 1923 eased Republican pressure on the North and allowed the new Northern Ireland parliament, which opened in June 1921, to establish effective control there. Sir James Craig, the first Prime Minster, repudiated the boundary commission and refused to budge an inch on boundary alterations. Derry was to remain in Northern Ireland. Furthermore, Unionists regained control of the city as electoral boundaries were re-drawn and proportional representation abolished.

15 *The Second World War*

During World War II it was vital for the allies to keep the supply routes and lines of communication open across the Atlantic. In this so-called "Battle of the Atlantic" the convoy system was introduced to provide maximum protection for allied shipping against German submarines. Naval bases from which escort vessels could operate were essential. Derry was one such base.

Derry had an ideal location. Not only was Derry an inland, deep-water port, providing safe anchorage in all weathers, she was also effectively beyond the range of German aircraft. In fact, during the whole war there was only one air raid on Derry. On the night of 15th April 1941 one lone bomber (out of 180 that bombed Belfast earlier in the evening), perhaps seeking the dockyard, dropped two mines (which fell short of their target) in Messines Park demolishing four houses and killing twelve people.

With Derry being such an important naval base, the threat of air raids was taken seriously. Balloon barrages were placed around the city to prevent attack by low-flying aircraft; anti-aircraft gun emplacements were built; and air-raid shelters were dug. The black-out procedure was enforced, with air-raid wardens patrolling the city to ensure no light could be seen from the outside. Throughout the war some people took the "blitz train" every evening to Buncrana in case of further raids. Others took to the countryside and slept in tents.

Derry was soon buzzing as a busy naval base, with ships berthed along the quay, others departing to meet up with convoys and others arriving at the end of a voyage. At the dolphin jetties, which were built at right angles to the quayside, destroyers were moored, sometimes five or six abreast. At Lisahally, by the long wooden wharf, built at the point where the river broadens into the Lough, scores of ships queued to refuel from the oil storage tanks.

By 30th June 1941 20,000 sailors of various nationalities - Norwegian, American, French, British, Canadian, Dutch and Russian - were based at the port. From the shipyard at Pennyburn to Craigavon Bridge, on both sides of the river, were moored from 150 to 200 warships. Derry was now a major allied naval base.

In April 1941, months before America entered the war, the U.S.A. handed over 50 old destroyers to the Royal Navy in return for the right to build four naval bases in Britain and Northern Ireland. On 31st June 1941 400 American civilian technicians arrived to begin construction work on a base in Derry, to be followed by another 600 in October. They built as their headquarters a three-storey building, of which two were below ground, protected with 15 feet of concrete, in the grounds of Magee College. In its plotting room a replica was made of the map in the map room at Derby House in Liverpool, from which Admiral Sir Max Horton directed the Battle of the Atlantic. From floor to ceiling a 30 feet high wall was covered with charts on which symbols could be placed, following the progress of the Atlantic convoys. It was to be used in the event of Derby House being put out of action. It was never needed.

As a communication centre, however, it was operational 24 hours a day, linking the naval base to the Coastal Command airfields throughout Northern Ireland and to the North-West Approaches Command at Derby House.

The base which the Americans spent 75 million dollars in constructing in Derry was the first U.S. advance base built in Europe. It was also the Americans' main naval radio station in the British Isles. The complex eventually consisted of communication bases at Rossdowney and Clooney, hospitals at Creevagh and Browning Drive and barracks at Springtown and Beechgrove.

To complement Derry's role as a naval base, airfields were built in the area to fly anti-submarine and convoy escort patrols. The construction of the aerodrome and runway at Eglinton created hundreds of jobs. It opened as a RAF Coastal Command base in August 1941 with 53 Squadron of Lockheed Hudsons operating from there. The airfield was soon transferred to Fighter Command. With such a large naval presence in the city, the newly arrived squadrons of Hurricanes, Mustangs and Spitfires were required to fly convoy escort patrols, and to defend the city in the event of an air raid. One of the squadrons flying from Eglinton was the American Eagle Squadron, known as 133 Squadron RAF. Formed in October 1941, before the US had officially entered the war, it consisted of American volunteers. When the Americans did enter the war, it was into Eglinton that the first US units flew. In May 1943 the airfield was loaned to the Royal Navy.

Maydown airfield was opened in 1942, and by the end of the war it was home to the Fleet Air Arm's largest squadron - 836 Naval Air Squadron. Maydown's principal role was to provide aircraft and personnel for merchant aircraft carriers. These converted merchant ships carried Swordfish biplanes which provided air cover for the Atlantic convoys. Barracudas, carrying torpedoes, also operated from here. By 1945 90 aircraft were operating from Maydown.

Protective patrols for convoys into and out of the Clyde and Mersey estuaries were provided by Lockheed Hudsons and Wellingtons operating from Limavady.

Of 25 German U-boats sunk during the war by aircraft operating out of Northern Ireland, 16 were destroyed by planes based at Ballykelly. 120 Squadron operating from here had, by the end of the war, RAF Coastal Command's highest tally of U-boats destroyed. In one week in October 1943 aircraft from this base sank 6 submarines.

The war brought a measure of prosperity to the city. The shirt factories were busy making trousers as well as shirts for the troops in the Middle East. The shipyard and long-established engineering firms such as Craigs and Browns carried out contract repair work for the Admiralty. Gales and high seas put an excessive strain upon escorts and destroyers in the North Atlantic. These vessels were subsequently brought into the city for repairs.

Derry was booming. Cafes, pubs, dance halls and cinemas were thronged with people. Most nights there were queues at her six picture houses. Smuggling, black marketing and thieving were rife, particularly of food and items of rations from army and navy stores. Whiskey, which just couldn't be got in the city, was smuggled in from across the border. One enterprising local smuggled bottles of whiskey inside a dead horse he was bringing from Buncrana to the knacker's yard in Derry.

With so many different nationalities in the city, there was certainly a lot of jealousy and conflict between the visiting forces and the local male population, between the British and the Americans and between white and black Americans. Many scuffles and fist fights broke out. One such fight occurred outside Littlewoods in Waterloo Place among 200 sailors of all nationalities. They fought their way up Waterloo Street, down Harvey Street, over Chamberlain Street and down William Street and back to where they started in Waterloo Place. The British and American shore patrols waded in with batons, but couldn't break it up. It took the

Royal Ulster Constabulary, who charged from three Crossley tenders, to end the fight, which had lasted 2 hours.

The choice of Derry for the surrender of the German U-boat fleet at Lisahally on 14th May 1945 was very symbolic, as throughout the war Derry had been home to up to 200 destroyers, corvettes, frigates, minesweepers and submarines.

These escort ships, together with aircraft from her nearby airfields, had protected many convoys across the Atlantic from the U-boat menace. Derry had played a vital role in the war effort.

When hostilities ended on 7th May 1945 the German U-boat fleet had been ordered to surface and radio their position. They were then disarmed and escorted to Lisahally by British, Canadian and American warships. Before being towed to sea and scuttled, there were up to 40 submarines, five abreast, moored along the wooden wharf at Lisahally.

16   *Free Derry*

In 1964 Captain Terence O'Neill, elected Prime Minister of Northern Ireland in 1963, declared: "My principal aims are to make Northern Ireland prosperous and to build bridges between the two traditions."

The 1960s seemed to bring a glimmer of hope on the economic and political fronts. For a while it looked as if Northern Ireland would become a world force in the man-made fibre industry. Courtaulds was the first man-made fibre firm to set up in Northern Ireland when it opened its Carrickfergus plant in 1948. When it was followed by other fibre companies in the 1950s and 1960s, including world leaders like Du Pont and Monsanto from America, ICI from Britain, British Enkalon from Holland and Hoechst from West Germany, they were heralded as the perfect modern replacement industry for the North's declining and outdated textile sector. By the end of the 1960s one-third of all man-made fibres produced in the United Kingdom came from Northern Ireland.

The IRA campaign of 1956 to 1962 had fizzled out, as it failed to arouse the support of Northern Ireland's Catholic community. Perhaps the most dramatic gesture towards reconciliation, however, was the exchange visits between the Northern Prime Minister Terence O'Neill and the Southern Taoiseach Sean Lemass in 1965.

The bugbear of local government reform, however, had not been dealt with. In Northern Ireland real power lay not at Stormont but in local government, as it controlled health, education, welfare, housing allocation and public employment recruitment. In February 1967 the Northern Ireland Civil Rights Association was formed to press for reform and, more specifically, for an end to gerrymandering, for a fair allocation of housing, for a fair distribution of local government jobs and for "one man, one vote" in local elections. With only householders being entitled to vote in local elections, this disfranchised proportionately more

Catholics than Protestants. The city of Derry now became an obvious focus for Civil Rights protests.

In the Derry City Council area the electoral wards were drawn up or gerrymandered in such a way as to ensure a Unionist majority on the Corporation, although Catholics made up 62% of the electorate. The city consisted of three wards, in each of which there was a straight vote to elect blocks of either Unionist or Nationalist councillors. In the elections of 1967 the North Ward, with a Protestant majority of 1,416, returned 8 Unionist councillors; the Waterside Ward, with a Protestant majority of 1,845, elected 4 Unionist councillors; while the South Ward, with a Catholic majority of 8,909, elected 8 Nationalist councillors. Thus the City Corporation consisted of 12 Unionist and 8 Nationalist councillors to represent 8,781 Protestant and 14,429 Catholic voters.

In 1968 the Civil Rights demonstrators took to the streets. On 5th October, despite a ban, a Civil Rights march in the city went ahead, only to find the way blocked by a line of the Royal Ulster Constabulary on Craigavon Bridge. The marchers, on turning to withdraw to the Waterside, found a line of police behind them. The RUC now baton-charged the demonstrators and dispersed them in the full view of television cameras. Derry and the Civil Rights movement had now grabbed the attention of the world's media. The O'Neill government now agreed to replace Derry City Council with a Development Commission.

On 3rd January 1969 violence flared in Derry again at the end of a People's Democracy march from Belfast, which had been ambushed at Burntollet Bridge, 7 miles from the city. In Guildhall Square police used armoured water cannons to disperse several hundred Catholics who had trapped Rev. Ian Paisley and his supporters in the Guildhall. A crowd shouting "We want Paisley" attacked the Guildhall with stones, breaking dozens of windows, but failing in their attempts to break through the wrought-iron gates.

Although O'Neill was re-elected Prime Minister on February 24th the dilemma he faced still remained: how to convince both the Catholics that he was serious about reform and his own Unionist grassroots that he would safeguard the Union with Great Britain. On April 29th O'Neill gave up the battle and resigned, his last speech as Prime Minister being to commend one man, one vote in local elections. James Chichester-Clark took over the premiership.

Tension was now building up, and the 12th August parade in Derry was to set the province on a course which no one seemed able to control. Chichester-Clark, despite predictions that violence would ensue, allowed the Apprentice Boys' parade to go ahead. On 12th August 1969 15,000 Apprentice Boys paraded to commemorate the 280th anniversary of the lifting of the siege imposed by James II in 1689. The parade began peacefully, but at 2.30 p.m., as it passed through the walled city, stone-throwing between groups of Catholics and Protestants started. The police responded by forcing the Catholic rioters down into the Bogside. Barricades appeared and petrol bombs were thrown. As police reinforcements arrived and took up positions the "Battle of the Bogside" began. Remembering what happened on April 19th when the RUC occupied the Bogside after rioting in the town, the Catholic community feared violence from the police if they were allowed to advance into the Bogside. For their part, the RUC feared Protestant property would be attacked if the Catholics broke out of the Bogside. For both sides it was crucial to hold their ground.

In the early evening the police drew up armoured cars and water cannon, and began to advance on the barricades of the Bogside. The police now produced a new weapon: they began to fire CS gas. After the first night's rioting 112 people were treated in hospital.

By the morning of Wednesday 13th August the battle had settled down into a ritual: the Bogsiders' stones and petrol bombs were answered by police CS gas. The mood in the Bogside was defiant, and the area was declared "Free Derry". The Derry Citizens Defence Association now demanded the withdrawal of the RUC and the abolishment of Stormont. That evening Jack Lynch, the Prime Minster of the Republic stated, "the Irish Government can no longer stand by and see innocent people injured and perhaps worse." To James Callaghan, the British Home Secretary, called urgently to the Home Office at 11 p.m., there seemed to be not only the possibility of civil war in the North, but also an invasion from the South.

On the 14th August, after 48 hours of continuous rioting, the Northern Ireland Government finally asked Westminster for help. Prime Minister Harold Wilson and Home Secretary James Callaghan agreed troops should be sent into Derry as a temporary emergency measure. At 5 p.m. on Thursday 14th August 400 soldiers of the First Battalion Prince of Wales Own Yorkshire Regiment crossed the Craigavon Bridge and entered the city. The troops were greeted with enthusiasm by the Catholics of the Bogside, as their arrival was seen as defeat of the RUC and of the Stormont government. It was felt Westminster would have to step in and the injustices of Unionist rule would be removed.

However, it wasn't that simple. Violence now spread to Belfast, and on the night of the 14th seven people were killed as hostile mobs clashed on the Catholic Lower Falls area. The vicious sectarian clashes continued through the 15th, with a further three people killed and 200 houses burnt. The British army was now also deployed in Belfast where it did manage to separate the two sides.

The events of these four days, 12th to 15th August 1969, totally polarised the two communities. The arrival of the army brought an uneasy peace, but already both communities had formed defence committees, organised at street level, and these were to be moulded during the summer and autumn into the Provisional IRA and the Ulster Defence Association. In 1969 Protestant hard-liners had already resurrected the Ulster Volunteer Force (named after Edward Carson's original Protestant army established in January 1913 to fight the Third Home Rule Bill) in response to the detente in North-South relations begun by Terence O'Neill in 1965. Internment without trial introduced in August 1971 and the killing of thirteen demonstrators in Derry by British paratroopers, only served to provide the IRA with new recruits. The Loyalist paramilitary response in the form of sectarian murders rapidly increased from 1972.

The events of 1968 and 1969 had by 1971 escalated into a sustained IRA campaign and the permanent presence of the British army in Northern Ireland.

17   A City Dreaming

Derry of the early 1960s was still to a large extent the city created by the phenomenal commercial and industrial growth of the 19th century. It was a compact city with housing, shops, commerce and industry all in close proximity to each other. From the 1960s the destruction of 19th century Derry, for better or worse, began. Derry's population was "confined and choked". Poor housing was replaced, which resulted in a dramatic physical expansion of the city.

Derry's traditional industries and even some of her new ones were in difficulties. In February 1967 the first of Derry's big city-centre shirt factories, namely the Star Factory, closed. Monarch Electric closed its factories at Bligh's Lane and Drumahoe with the loss of 900 jobs in January 1967. Derry's unemployment rate now stood at 20% with one third of young men "idle".

In the 1970s and early 1980s Derry's greatest tragedy was the combined effect of the Troubles and her economic decline. Towards the end of the 1980s, however, light was beginning to appear at the end of the tunnel.

From the mid-1980s more modern developments were beginning to contribute to the regeneration and revitalisation of the city. Nineteen eighty-four saw the opening of the Richmond Shopping Centre in June and the Foyle Bridge in October of that year.

To enable Derry to recapture its former position as the Regional Centre of the North West, the Department of the Environment for Northern Ireland drew up development concepts – 'City of Derry Real Estate Opportunity' – that it felt were worthy of private investment.

The fruits of these efforts were rewarded on 18th December 1989 when Minister of the Economy, Richard Needham announced plans for the £65 million Foyleside, a major city-centre shopping development located between the old City Wall and the River Foyle, in association with

O'Connell Development Company of Boston. Work began on Foyleside on 1st June 1993 and it opened its doors to shoppers on 25th September 1995.

The 1990s saw a transformation in Derry's fortunes, brought about by a combination of public sector, private sector and community-led initiatives. One commentator stated that the bomb sites of the 70s were replaced with the building sites of the 90s.

President of the United States, William J Clinton, when he spoke at Guildhall Square on 30th November 1995, captured the mood of Derry's renewed confidence: "I believe we live in a time of hope and history rhyming. Standing here in front of the Guildhall, looking over these historic walls, I see a peaceful city, a hopeful city, full of young people that should have a peaceful and prosperous future here where their roots and families are."

The 1990s saw Derry's transport network enhanced by a new deep-water port at Lisahally and the upgrading of Eglinton airport. On 10th July 1990 Secretary of State, Peter Brooke, announced details of a new £13 million deep-water port at Lisahally. At midnight on 19th February 1993 the City centre docks officially closed, after 139 years in operation. Business was now transferred, four miles downstream, to Lisahally Port with 365 metres of quayside and access through an eight-metre deep Lough Foyle channel.

The transformation of Eglinton airport, which Derry City Council acquired in 1978, was also seen as crucial in establishing Derry as a regional hub. March 1994 saw the official opening of City of Derry Airport following an £11 million redevelopment programme involving new passenger terminal facilities and the upgrade and extension of runways.

As Derry, with a population of over 107,000 and a hinterland of 350,000, entered the new Millennium there was no doubt that it was regaining its vitality. Tourism and the safeguarding and redevelopment of historic buildings were now seen as key components of urban regeneration. In all these plans revitalisation of the riverfront is a key objective; to re-establish the connections between the City Centre and the River.

In 2003 the Historic Walled City of Derry was designated by Northern Ireland Tourist Board as one of five Signature Tourism Projects for Northern Ireland offering a 'world class visitor experience'. Derry is the only remaining walled city in the British Isles, and its perfectly preserved walls are one of the finest examples of their kind in Europe.

In July 2003 Ilex was established as the Urban Regeneration Company for the Derry City Council area. Its remit: to plan, develop, coordinate and sustain the economic, physical and social regeneration of the Derry City Council area by engaging both the private and public sector; with specific responsibility to redevelop the two former military bases of Ebrington and Fort George.

Ebrington Barracks, which closed in 2003, on the east bank of the River Foyle, was built in 1841 in the shape of a star, with buildings on three sides overlooking the city and the River Foyle. The centre piece of the Star Fort is the former parade ground, with broad vistas to the west across the River Foyle.

In September 2010, Ilex awarded a £6 million contract for development of the parade ground into a new public square. On 14th February 2012, the city's newest public space, measuring 26 acres, which is bigger than Trafalgar Square, London was opened by the First Minister, Peter Robinson and Deputy First Minister, Martin McGuinness. Peter Robinson proclaimed that a 'massive transformation' was taking place in Derry.

Key to the regeneration of Ebrington was the creation of a new foot and cycle bridge, 312 metres long, to connect the Waterside with the city centre. Derry's 'Peace Bridge', costing £14 million and funded by the European Union Peace III programme under the Shared Space initiative, was officially opened to the public on Saturday 25th June 2011. Sir Roy McNulty, chairman of Ilex, claimed that the Peace Bridge, a symbolic union of what was once a divided city, will become the city's iconic image.

Inspired by Liverpool's huge success as European Capital of Culture in 2008, the Government launched a UK City of Culture competition to enable the host city to devise a programme of events and projects which reflects its identity, showcases its culture and raises its profile, opening the doors to increased private investment, regeneration, tourism and free publicity through media coverage.

On 15th July 2010, it was announced that Derry~Londonderry, chosen from an original list of 29, was to become UK's first ever City of Culture in 2013. Recognition of the power of culture to bring people together was the key to Derry's winning bid.

At the programme launch, Shona McCarthy, Chief Executive of Culture Company 2013 said: "We hope that Derry~Londonderry's City of Culture year brings a sense of joy, a sense of ambition, a sense of pride in our community, a sense of being part of a global community, and in the end a sense of achievement – that we all did this together and it meant something. A huge success for a small city."

In the previous year, 2012, Derry had demonstrated its capacity to host and organise major international events with a maritime festival to celebrate the arrival of the Clipper Round the World Yacht Race; over 10 days, from 29th June to 8th July 2012, the festival drew over 100,000 people to Queen's Quay. The Clipper Race and its associated Foyle Maritime Festival returned to Derry in summers of 2014, 2016 and 2018.

The founder and chairman of the Clipper Round the World Yacht Race, Sir Robin Knox-Johnston said: "I think Derry has been one of the most successful stop overs ever and I think the reason for that is that the whole city seems to have become involved in the event." He continued, the city "is saying to the world: 'This is the new Londonderry…this is the new Northern Ireland, this is the new Ireland come and have a look because it's a great place'."

On 23rd October 2012, *Lonely Planet* ranked Derry fourth in the best cities in the world to visit in 2013. The guide says: "Londonderry is the UK City of Culture 2013, which means this vibrant historic walled city is undergoing a renaissance…Derry is a brilliant example of a city that has bounced back from difficult times. This is a city with heart, which shines through in its exciting arts and music scene."

Derry's 'heart' was clearly visible to the world when an expectant crowd packed Guildhall Square on 15th June 2010 to hear British Prime Minister, David Cameron, rise in the House of Commons, to state that the shooting of 13 civil rights marchers on Bloody Sunday, 30th January 1972, was "unjustified and unjustifiable". An apology followed, when on behalf of the government and the country he said, "I am deeply sorry".

The Saville Inquiry, the longest independent public inquiry in British legal history, which opened in April 1998 and heard evidence from 610 soldiers, 729 civilians, 30 journalists, 20 government officials and 53 police officers, accepted that the victims of Bloody Sunday were innocent. As far as the families of the victims were concerned "the truth has been brought home at last."

With an expected opening in spring 2020, a maritime museum is set to become one of the key features of a revitalised Ebrington Square. The new facility, given planning approval in November 2017, will celebrate the city's and Lough Foyle's historic maritime importance, including its role as a vital naval base during the Battle of the Atlantic in the Second World War, and as a gateway to North America for merchants and emigrants.

Derry City and Strabane District Council (established 1 April 2015) see it as an important flagship scheme for the riverfront site – it will provide a much-needed catalyst for the physical and economic regeneration of Ebrington, the city and region. The proposal is to alter and extend a number of former military buildings, including the original military hospital, built 1841, on north side of the parade ground, to provide a maritime museum and archive centre.

Local politician, Mark H. Durkan said, "I welcome this planning decision as another piece in the Ebrington jigsaw. On the back of other recent developments and approvals on the site, it is becoming clear that the huge potential of this key site can be realised."

In February 2017, Niche Drinks secured planning permission to convert four buildings, including the barrack jail and guardhouse, on south side of Ebrington Square, into a whiskey distillery and visitor centre. The Quiet Man Craft Distillery will be the first whiskey distillery to operate in the city in nearly 100 years. Derry has a proud whiskey distilling tradition. Watt's Distillery in Abbey Street, in its heyday producing 1.5 million gallons annually of their flagship brand, *The Tyrconnel Whiskey*, had closed its doors in October 1921.

In November 2017, a planning application was lodged for a new 152-bedroom hotel, to be known as 'The Ebrington', on east flank of Ebrington Square, across five of the former army buildings, including the existing Clock Tower Building, originally built in 1841 as accommodation blocks.

On 2nd January 2018 *The Irish News* reported that five years on from the year-long celebration of culture, music and the arts in Derry~Londonderry as UK City of Culture 2013, the city's image has been transformed. Before 2013, according to former Mayor of the city, Martin Reilly, Derry was better known as the birthplace of the Troubles while now it is looked on as a key tourist attraction.

The Observer of Sunday 29th December 2013 reported that "Derry's year as UK city of culture reawakened the voice of idealism" and that the "city's moment in the artistic spotlight has given it the chance to look forward, without forgetting its past."

Paul Greengrass, film director, stated, "Derry's problems, apart from the obvious, have been geographical; at the edge of the kingdom and the edge of Ireland. Once the shirt factories had gone, economic isolation was part of that remoteness, so that not long ago it was hard to say to a young person in Derry, 'You should stay'. I know it's easy to be optimistic from the outside, but there's a chance now you'd win the argument and persuade them to remain."

Broadcaster, Gerry Anderson described the City of Culture project in *The Irish Times* in June 2012 as "probably the best thing that ever happened to the city". In describing his home city he said, "it's an international city, we have a port; we get a lot of foreign visitors. But we're very parochial at the same time. Almost everyone has a grandmother who moved here from Donegal to work in the shirt factories…Derry is like an independent statelet, I suppose. It's Monaco without the money."

Gerry Anderson concluded in his 2014 film homage to Derry, directed by Mark McCauley, entitled *A City Dreaming*: "Now I see a people with positivity and energy in their hearts. I hope they're right."